Crucial Issues in Testing

THE NATIONAL SOCIETY
FOR THE STUDY OF EDUCATION

Series on Contemporary Educational Issues
Kenneth J. Rehage, Series Editor

The 1974 Titles

Conflicting Conceptions of Curriculum, Elliot Eisner and Elizabeth
  Vallance, Editors
Crucial Issues in Testing, Ralph W. Tyler and Richard M. Wolf,
  Editors
Cultural Pluralism, Edgar G. Epps, Editor
Rethinking Educational Equality, Andrew Kopan and Herbert
  Walberg, Editors

The National Society for the Study of Education also publishes Yearbooks which are distributed by the University of Chicago Press. Inquiries regarding all publications of the Society, as well as inquiries
about membership in the Society, may be addressed to the Secretary-
Treasurer, 5835 Kimbark Avenue, Chicago, 60637.

Crucial Issues
in
Testing

Edited by

Ralph W. Tyler

Director Emeritus
Center for Advanced Study in the Behavioral Sciences

and

Richard M. Wolf

Associate Professor of Psychology and Education
Teachers College, Columbia University

McCutchan Publishing Corporation
2526 Grove Street
Berkeley, California 94704

ISBN 8211-1714-9
Library of Congress Catalog Card Number 73-20855

© 1974 by McCutchan Publishing Corporation
Printed in the United States of America

Series Foreword

In recent years much discussion has centered around the use of tests in the educational enterprise. Such discussions will surely continue. Ralph W. Tyler and Richard M. Wolf kindly accepted our invitation to prepare a volume that would identify some of the critical issues in testing to which attention must certainly be given in the years immediately ahead. In addition to their own original essays, Tyler and Wolf have selected some previously published works of others to be included in this volume. The book as a whole thus provides an excellent background against which further consideration of the issues surrounding testing can take place.

Crucial Issues in Testing is one of four titles in the 1974 Series on Contemporary Educational Issues published in paperback format under the auspices of the National Society for the Study of Education. Other titles in the Series are: *Conflicting Conceptions of Curriculum*, edited by Elliot Eisner and Elizabeth Vallance; *Cultural Pluralism*, edited by Edgar G. Epps; *Rethinking Educational Equality*, edited by Herbert Walberg and Andrew Kopan.

With this new set of four volumes the Society continues a program, begun in 1971, of bringing out timely books that will provide a background for informed discussion of critical issues in education.

Kenneth J. Rehage

for the Committee on the Expanded
Publication Program of the
National Society for the Study
of Education

Contributors

Peter W. Airasian, Associate Professor of Education, Boston College

Scarvia Anderson, Executive Director for Special Development, Educational Testing Service

Henry S. Dyer, Educational Testing Service

Carmen J. Finley, American Institute for Research (Palo Alto)

Edmund W. Gordon, Professor of Education, Teachers College, Columbia University

George H. Johnson, Associate Staff Director, National Assessment of Educational Progress

George F. Madaus, Professor of Education, Boston College

Samuel Messick, Vice president, Research, Educational Testing Service

Elsa Rosenthal, Educational Testing Service

Robert L. Thorndike, Professor of Education, Teachers College, Columbia University

Ralph W. Tyler, Director Emeritus, Center for Advanced Study in the Behavioral Sciences

Robert L. Williams, Director, Black Studies Program, Washington University, St. Louis

Richard M. Wolf, Associate Professor of Psychology and Education, Teachers College, Columbia University

Contents

Introduction

A Perspective on the Issues

Ralph W. Tyler

In 1969 the National Society for the Study of Education devoted its Sixty-eighth Yearbook, Part II, to educational evaluation. That yearbook provides a useful perspective for examining the crucial issues in testing that are apparent today, and, in the introductory chapter, I commented that,

Since World War II, and particularly during the past decade, profound changes have been taking place in educational evaluation. This yearbook reviews some of these developments and seeks to assess their significance for both educational theory and practice.

New concepts, new procedures, and new instruments of evaluation are emerging from the interaction among new needs for educational evaluation, new conditions that must be met, new knowledge about education, and new technologies that can be utilized. As an example of this interaction, most theories of testing and evaluation have been developed on the assumption that the primary uses for tests and other evaluative devices are to measure individual differences and to furnish reliable estimates of the mean scores for groups of persons. The theories formulated to guide practice under this assumption have emphasized homogeneity of test content and the concentration of item difficulties near the 50-percent point. Since Sputnik, massive financial support has been given to projects concerned with the development of new courses in science and mathematics. Those supporting the construction of the new courses and teachers and administrators who are considering the use of them in their schools are asking for an evaluation of the effectiveness of the courses in comparison with other courses in the same fields. Most tests on the market were not constructed to furnish relative appraisals of different courses, and they have been found inadequate for the task. This need for evaluation of courses and curriculums is stimulating the development of new procedures, instruments, and theories that are designed to meet the need.

Similarly, Title I of the Elementary and Secondary Education Act of 1965 authorizes nearly $1 billion to be allotted to schools with a high concentration of children from homes in poverty, and the Act requires each local district receiving such funds to evaluate the effectiveness of the educational efforts thus supported. Many schools and a majority of the states reported that they had no means readily available for conducting such evaluative studies. This led to the establishment of several centers that are developing new theories and procedures for evaluating Title I activities.

A third illustration of the influence of new needs is the demand being made by influential groups of citizens for appraisals that will furnish sound data to guide educational improvement. The statement of July 1968, by the Research and Policy Committee of the Committee for Economic Development is a case in point. It reads:

> Innovation in education, whether it involves the use of new curriculum materials or new educational technology, has become essential if the schools are to be genuinely effective in achieving their aims and goals. Continuing assessment of the product of the schools also is necessary. This means the development of principles and techniques for critically judging the worth of whatever the schools teach and the effectiveness and efficiency of their methods of instruction.[1]

The recent rapid increase in the number and availability of technological devices in education, such as television, tape recorders, and computers, has brought to attention the need to evaluate the effectiveness of these devices for various kinds of educational tasks. Traditional test theory has not been sufficiently relevant to design evaluative studies of technological devices, nor have the available achievement tests been satisfactory for this purpose. The effort to appraise some of these devices has led to new developments in evaluation.

The changes in American society are creating new conditions for education that frequently require new types of evaluation in order to obtain valid appraisals appropriate to the new conditions. For example, the applications of science and technology in agriculture, industry, defense, commerce, and the health services have shifted the nature of human occupations from those based largely on physical strength and manual dexterity to those involving large components of intellectual activity and social sensitivity and skills. Very few young people who have not attained the functional literacy represented by the average achievement of students at the end of the fifth grade can find jobs.

At the other extreme, the great employment opportunities are in science, engineering, education, the health services, recreation services, social services, management, and accounting. In our time, the role of the school has shifted from that of selecting out a small percent of the pupils for more advanced education (while the others dropped out and went to work) to that of effectively reaching every child to enable him to go on learning far beyond the expected level of twenty-five years ago. The task of the college is not to find a favored few but to identify a wide range of potential talents and to help each student realize this potential both for his own self-realization and in order to meet the ever increasing demands of a complex technological society. These changed conditions are stimulating the development of new instruments and new procedures of educational evaluation.

Another illustration of the changing conditions affecting the theory, procedures, and instruments of evaluation is afforded by the current stress upon improving the educational opportunities of disadvantaged children. Recent studies of achievement testing of children in poverty have shown that the test items do not include a reliable sample of things being learned by most disadvantaged children. Furthermore, interviews with the children revealed that the language of most tests was such that many poor children and many from the disadvantaged minority groups did not understand what they were asked to do in responding to each test question. Efforts to meet the need for appraising the educational progress of disadvantaged children are producing new ideas and new means of educational evaluation.

New knowledge about education is also influencing evaluation. For example, the recent findings of many studies regarding the powerful effects of the student's home culture and community environment upon his learning have clarified the need for evaluating these factors in order to guide and improve education. New theories were necessary to rationalize procedures for appraising home and community environment and new instruments had to be developed.

As another illustration, a series of investigations like those of Newcomb and Coleman have shown the strong influence of peer-group attitudes, practices, and interests upon the learning of its members.[2] These investigations have also shown the need for evaluating the nature, direction, and amount of peer-group influences in developing effective school programs.

The emergence of new technologies has also strongly influenced developments in educational evaluation. The high-speed electronic computer is the most obvious illustration of an emerging technology that is, in many respects, revolutionizing evaluation. The computer has made possible the recording and storage of complex data of many types in a way that permits nearly instantaneous retrieval and processing. This capability has strengthened the interest of evaluators in large-scale studies of individual performance involving large numbers of variables, and new theories, procedures, and instruments are being developed.

The technology of high-fidelity recording and reproduction of sound has influenced the range of objectives appraised and the devices used in the fields of language and music, and it has aided the standardization of group-test administration by permitting the substitution of a tape recording for the directions given by a local proctor. These two examples represent only a fraction of the new technologies that are currently influencing developments in educational evaluation.[3]

Educational Testing—Then and Now

Educational testing became institutionalized in America at a time when society and the educational system differed in several important respects from that of today. During World War I the psychological testing used to select those who could quickly learn to be officers and technical personnel from the two million men enlisted in the military service impressed not only the psychologists of that day but also leaders in education, business, and civic affairs. Schools, colleges, and large industrial organizations were seen as the proper civilian settings for the initiation and development of testing, and educational institutions and the personnel departments of industrial organizations were engaged to select and sort persons. Since tests had proved useful in selecting and sorting military personnel, it seemed that similar tests could be developed for civilian conditions, and for children and youth as well as young adults.

Educational testing thus began as a means for selecting and sorting pupils, and the principles and practices of testing that have been worked out since 1918 are largely the refining of means to serve these functions rather than other educational purposes. They are based upon the psychology of individual differences rather than upon the psychology of learning. This was an appropriate development under the societal conditions of the time.

When most people were employed in unskilled or semiskilled labor and only 5 percent were in professional or managerial occupations, most workers could survive with little or no formal education. Only a few needed a college education in their work. Under such conditions, an accepted function of schools and colleges was to sort children and youth, eliminating the least promising for further education and encouraging the few qualified to go on. The lock-step progress of instruction and the grading system used were developed to sort students rather than to help each one get an education. By moving the whole class at the same rate from topic to topic, pacing the movement in accord with the performance of the average student, those with more difficulty in learning would gradually drop back and eventually stop trying. This process was reinforced by a grading system that gave low marks to those having difficulty, further discouraging them, and high marks to those who learned easily and quickly, thus encouraging them to continue their formal education.

These policies and practices have existed for so long that we rarely note how sharply they differ from those of an institution devoted wholly to teaching and learning. For example, if you or I want to learn to play golf, we go to a golf "pro" whose job it is to teach us. We do not expect that after a few practice periods he will say, "You are getting a 'D' in your work. I may have to fail you if you don't improve." Instead, we expect him to say "You are making progress on your drive, but you need to bring your full body into the swing. A little later I'll give you further practice on your putting to increase accuracy and decrease power." An institution concerned primarily with learning and teaching follows practices based on the available knowledge of how people learn. Schools and colleges, in contrast, are only partly concerned with helping each student learn. They are also likely to be preoccupied with grading, classifying, and other sorting functions. Testing was adopted and developed as a tool for performing these functions. So-called intelligence tests were used for initial sorting, and they indicated, for teachers and for parents, the likely success of children in the educational system. Later, as the concept of intelligence widened in scope, the term "aptitude tests" was applied to examinations devised to aid in this preliminary classification and guidance. Achievement tests were developed to indicate a student's progress in school as compared to other students.

This sufficed in a society where the positions available for the occupational, social, and political elite were few in number. Schools and colleges were a major means for rationing educational opportunities to conform to the social structure. It seemed sensible then to give everyone a chance to jump the hurdles and to record the results, and to report them in a way that would encourage students, and their parents, to seek further educational opportunities only as success in the competition of previous years was achieved.

Today we have a different situation. By the use of science and technology we are meeting our nation's need for food and fiber using only 5 percent of the labor force. Less than 5 percent is employed as nonfarm, unskilled labor. Less than 40 percent of our total labor force is employed in producing and distributing material goods. More than 60 percent is furnishing nonmaterial services—health services, educational services, various social services, recreational services, accounting and administrative services—for which there is an ever-rising demand. A young person who has not completed elementary education can find very few jobs. Employment in fields that are growing requires at least a high school education. The critical task is no longer to sort students but, rather, to educate a much larger proportion of students to meet current opportunities.

As education has become essential for almost everyone in order to participate constructively in contemporary society, many more people have become actively concerned about the educational opportunities available to them and their children. Community involvement has become a guideline for many state and federal educational programs. Minority groups are putting pressure on colleges and universities to furnish opportunities for their members. Along with this wider interest in education, increasing attention is being directed toward policies and practices that appear to restrict the educational opportunities of certain social classes, racial and ethnic groups, and individuals. Since tests are commonly used in schools and colleges to obtain data used in admissions, sorting, and guidance, they have become the focus of controversy in connection with efforts of various groups to obtain greater educational opportunities.

Issues in Testing—Some Current Contexts

There are several contexts in which testing issues arise. First, the Civil Rights Movement, which gained great attention following the Supreme Court decision on school segregation in 1954, brought into sharp focus issues raised earlier by Allison Davis in his study of intelligence testing. How, it was asked, could equal educational opportunity be provided for minority groups if the access to educational institutions, programs, or courses was controlled by tests whose form, vocabulary, content, and means of motivation were less appropriate for or familiar to minority groups than white middle-class students? How equal was educational opportunity if pupils were placed within the school in "streams" or so-called "ability groups" based on test results that discriminated against certain classes of individuals? How many teachers would seek to identify the strengths of each pupil in order to direct his educational efforts if they believed that test reports provided a dependable picture of the "real abilities" of the children? Would not most of them interpret the test reports in ways that made them self-fulfilling prophecies? How many pupils would continue to have confidence in their ability and put forth a strong effort to succeed in their school endeavors if their test scores were low? Questions like these have stimulated inquiry as well as controversy on the impact of testing on minority groups.

A second context involves the effort to make education more effective in reaching all children and youth. Earlier mention was made of the effect of programs designed for the "average student" when those who are having more difficulty in learning fail to achieve satisfactory results. The practice of so-called ability grouping, in which pupils are grouped into two or more classes for differential instruction, largely on the basis of test results, is similarly attacked as a procedure that guarantees limited learning on the part of children placed in "low-ability groups." Programs seeking to individualize instruction, like the Individually Prescribed Instruction designed by the University of Pittsburgh Learning Research and Development Center, use placement, diagnostic, and mastery tests that are criterion-referenced rather than norm-referenced. Similarly, in their work on mastery learning programs, Benjamin S. Bloom and his colleagues find the usual achievement tests inappropriate for appraising the learning of students under conditions that seek to maximize the proportion of students who "master" the essentials of the course.

Another context in which issues have arisen is that of assessing educational institutions. Achievement tests were designed to appraise individuals in terms of their deviations from the mean of the population to which they belong. The score usually reported for an achievement test is an abstract number that has no concrete reference. It is usually derived from a number which is the sum of the number of exercises answered correctly. Thus it is two steps removed from reporting what tasks the individual has performed correctly. If typical achievement tests are employed to appraise the educational accomplishments of a school or school system by using the mean or average score of the students, this is yet a third step removed from the actual performance of individual students on particular test exercises. Comparisons can be made with the mean score of the norming population of students and with mean scores of other groups, but these calculations do not answer questions about what students have learned. Furthermore, the method of constructing the test to maximize items that reveal individual differences among students makes it impossible to answer questions about what all or nearly all students have learned and what important things have been learned by only a small percentage. The exercises on such tests are not selected to form a representative sample of what students have learned. Instead, they are a sample of items that clearly differentiate among students. Since the purpose of assessing schools or school systems is to ascertain what various populations of students are learning, so-called criterion-referenced tests are being constructed to serve this purpose more directly than the norm-referenced tests.

The effort to appraise institutions rather than individuals involves problems of sampling populations and subpopulations of students enrolled in the institutions. To make an efficient assessment of the learning of students within an institution does not require that every student be tested if a representative and reliable sample of students can be selected for testing. This procedure raises some technical issues that are currently being studied. The sampling problems are different from those commonly considered by test specialists. Criterion-referenced tests require representative and adequate samples of each of the major things that students are expected to learn, and efficient population sampling procedure requires representative and adequate samples of each population or subpopulation of students in the institution. The first requirement results in many more exercises than are commonly included in a norm-referenced test because the latter test can obtain a representative and adequate sample of items that differentiate among students using very few items from each of the divisions of things to be learned. The requirement that a representative and adequate sample of each population or subpopulation of students enrolled in the institution be utilized usually results in a great reduction in the number of students responding to each exercise in comparison with the practice in norm-referenced testing, in which everyone is usually included because of the use of these tests to compare individual students.

A fourth context in which issues have arisen is that of measuring the relative effectiveness of different educational programs, teaching methods, or instructional materials. In the past this kind of evaluation has been commonly made by using commercially available achievement tests. Quite typically these appraisals reveal no reliable differences between the experimental program, method, or materials and those that serve as controls or bases of comparison. The recent reexamination of tests and testing has, however, raised questions regarding the appropriateness of the tests used for purposes of appraisal. Usually a new program, method, or instructional material is designed to overcome a recognized difficulty encountered in the "old" program, method, or material. This difficulty is likely to be that certain groups of pupils are not being reached, or that progress is being made toward certain but not all important educational objectives, or that the instructional system is not being properly managed. The overall achievement tests provide only a small number of exercises that sample difficulties in learning encountered by certain groups of students, or certain particular educational objectives, or the portions of the course where instructional management is critical. Hence, it is being argued that typical achievement tests do not have the necessary precision and focus to measure the differences that might arise from new programs, methods, or materials.

A fifth context is the current concern with maintaining individual privacy in certain areas of life in spite of the close interdependence of people in economic, political, and civic affairs. The content of tests in the cognitive domain has not usually been questioned. Attitude scales, personality inventories, and personal social adjustment questionnaires have been attacked, however, on the ground that pupils are asked questions about feelings and actions that should be protected as private and not subject to public scrutiny. Also, some questions asked on the face sheets of tests regarding such family matters as the income, occupation, and education of parents are considered by some to be an invasion of privacy. In order to protect the private lives of individuals from the probing of school personnel, employers, social workers, or behavioral scientists, new standards for testing are emerging. The subjects at issue are not only whether test results and answer sheets should be publicly available but also whether it is proper for questions to be asked about matters that are generally considered private.

In these five contexts (the drive to extend civil rights to all segments of American society; the growing efforts to make education effective for all children and youth; the call for assessment of educational institutions; the need to appraise new educational programs, methods, and instructional materials; and the concern for protecting the private life of the individual in this interdependent, increasingly crowded society) testing is being critically examined. New issues have arisen, and old ones have been revived in the painful process of aligning and developing policies and practices that are consistent with the contemporary situation in our society. This volume is a representative collection of discussions now under way.

Notes

1. *Innovation in Education: New Directions for the American School* (New York: Committee for Economic Development, 1968), 13.

2. See Theodore M. Newcomb, "The General Nature of Peer Group Influence," in Theodore M. Newcomb and Everett K. Wilson (eds.), *College Peer Group* (Chicago: Aldine Publishing Co., 1966), 2-16; see also James S. Coleman, "Peer Cultures and Education in Modern Society," *ibid.*, 244-69.

3. Ralph W. Tyler, "Introduction," in *Educational Evaluation: New Roles, New Means,* Sixty-eighth Yearbook of the National Society for the Study of Education, Part II (Chicago: University of Chicago Press, 1969), 1-4.

Part One
Testing and Minority Groups

The issues involved in testing individuals from minority groups are theoretically and methodologically complex, as well as being highly emotionally charged. Criticisms of testing procedures used for members of minority groups have come from many quarters and have been made on various grounds in recent years. One issue involves whether tests that were supposedly designed for a majority group can legitimately be administered to a culturally different group. It has been argued that the backgrounds of test makers and the nature of the procedures followed in the construction of tests preclude the development of tests that can legitimately be used for members of minority groups. Further, tests are sometimes viewed as devices created by a majority group to perpetuate the lower status of the minority group. In the following article Robert Williams questions the legitimacy of using conventional ability and achievement tests with minority group members.

A second issue in the testing of minority group members involves the content of specific items in a test. Individuals with different experiential backgrounds can be expected to come to a testing situation differently prepared to answer the questions contained in a test. If the different experiential backgrounds of the individuals arise out of their membership in culturally diverse groups, then the appropriateness of various test items for use with such individuals can be questioned. This point is forcefully made by Williams, as well as Messick and Anderson, and Thorndike.

While the above criticisms have frequently been lodged, recent attention has focused on the use of test results rather than on the tests themselves. It is here that one is immediately faced with a problem of definition. What constitutes fairness in a test? What is bias? How can it be determined? These are issues that Thorndike addresses. While his argument is somewhat technical, it is important to follow Thorndike's development of the issue of cultural fairness not only because of its centrality but because it reveals the fundamental dilemma facing educators who wish to make the fairest possible use of test information in making decisions involving members of minority groups.

1. Black Pride, Academic Relevance, and Individual Achievement

Robert I. Williams

The purpose of this chapter is to provide a new perspective aimed at understanding the ability and academic achievement of Black students. It is no accident that the general impression held by many American citizens is that Black Americans are inferior to whites in intelligence. It is also not surprising to find that comparative research of Black and white Americans promotes the "holier than thou image." Comparative research encourages racist thinking. It is more appropriate to look at the unique resources and strengths of each group rather than to focus on the differences.

Typical of the research studies comparing Black and white Americans is the statement found in a recent letter to the editor of *Science*. The letter on "Racial Differences" states that in "the general population, Negroes have a distribution of intelligence . . . that has a mean approximately one standard deviation below the Caucasian mean."[1]

Earlier this year I attempted to correct the distortion and confusion regarding Black and white intelligence:

Studies have repeatedly shown that Black people do not have inferior intelligence. What white researchers have repeatedly shown is that the IQ as contrasted

Reprinted with permission from *The Counseling Psychologist*, 2 (No, 1, 1970), 18-21.

with intelligence is one standard deviation below the Caucasian mean. There is a clear and definite difference between intelligence, *per se,* and the concept of the intelligence quotient, or IQ. The latter is measured as relative intelligence, not absolute, and contains considerable error in measurement, whereas the former. indicates the extent to which an individual is able to understand and adapt to his environment.[2]

Responding to my criticism, L. G. Humphreys wrote the following:

You are making some potentially serious mistakes in my opinion, both psychologically and with respect to the welfare of black citizens. When you set up a concept of "real" intelligence as something inside the organism, you are playing into the hands of racists. Where does "real" intelligence come from, if not from genetics? I define intelligence as the repertoire of intellectual skills and knowledge available to a person at any one period of time. Intelligence is defined by a consensus as illustrated by the Binet and the Wexler [sic].[3]

It is unfortunate that such a position is advanced by such a reputable test and measurement psychologist. I take the opposite position that *intelligence* cannot be properly defined as a consensus of opinion. Further, it is important that the two concepts—intelligence and IQ—not be used interchangeably.

Jensen lapses into language which confuses the distinctions between IQ and intelligence. He states:

Much of my paper is a review of the methods and evidence that lead me to the conclusion that individual differences in intelligence—that is IQ—are predominantly attributable to genetic differences, with minor environmental factors contributing a minor portion of the variance among individuals in IQ. The heritability of IQ . . . comes out to about 80%.[4]

There is an erroneous equation made between IQ and intelligence; this error leads the general population to the false conclusion that Blacks are inferior to whites in ability. Moreover, it is ridiculous to think of inheriting an IQ — which is nothing more than a set of scores earned on a test.

Thomas Gray, a poet, once wrote, "Full many a flower is born to blush unseen and waste its sweetness on the desert air." This paper is concerned with the fact that millions of Black people will live out their lives under desert circumstances and blush unseen. Obstacles have been placed in the way of their attainment of personal, social, and economic goals. It is no accident that the focus of most research studies has been on the victims rather than the victimizers, the oppressed rather than the oppressors, the colonized rather than the settlers, the deprived rather than the deprivers, and the disadvantaged rather than the disadvantagers. It is high time that the focus be shifted to the causes rather than the results. Henry David Thoreau / once said, "There are many hacking away at the branches of evil but not one getting to the roots of the problem."

Thus, it is important that studies now be aimed at the causes of Moynihanism, Jensenism, Styronism, and Benign Neglectism. It is important that the reader know that I, Robert L. Williams, Ph.D., have an IQ of 82 as measured by standardized intelligence tests. It is important to know that I was counseled not to enter college because of my "poor ability." It was suggested that I become an auto mechanic because I was good with my hands, not my mind. What does this mean? It means that I was one of the flowers "born to blush unseen"; a John Milton unable to see the beauty of himself reflected in the mirror. As Waring Cunly, a Black poet, wrote, "She does not know her beauty. She thinks her brown body has no glory. . . . And dishwater gives back no images."/

I must remind you, however, that measured IQ in Black people is not an accurate measure of intelligence. An example is necessary here. Let us take two track stars, Runner A and Runner B. The results show that Runner A is clocked in the 100 yard dash at 10.0 seconds flat with the help of a 25 mile per hour tailwind. Runner B is clocked at 10.2 seconds running against a 25 mile per hour wind. My question is, who is the better runner? When we talk about individual achievement, we must look at the conditions under which students are performing. If my 82 IQ was sufficient to make it through a doctoral program (in Psychology) at Washington University, then that IQ must be the equivalent of 130 or above. What I am saying is that the measures of individual achievement and the conditions confronting the learner are different for Blacks and whites.

It has been assumed for a number of years that Black children have no "verbal skills," or, at best, have some difficulty in articulation. That allegation is absolutely not true. What is really being said is that those verbal skills unique to the Black community are not rewarded in the middle-class classroom. For example, many Black children play "The Dozens" and play it quite well. "The Dozens" refers to the game of verbal insults against another person's parents. I have known Black students who were masters at playing "The Dozens" but could not read. They could phrase their "Dozens" in iambic pentameter with no difficulty and create such an emotional stir in their listener that there was no question about their verbal superiority. The average Black child has learned long poems such as "The Signifying Monkey," "Shine," and "The Pool Shooting Monkey." There never has been any question in my mind about the ability of these students to engage in verbal battles or in dialogues with their colleagues. Nor has there ever been a question of memory; the problem has been that these bits of classical Black poetry and prose are not reinforced in the schoolroom. The Black child has had to leave his culture and verbal skills outside the door of the classroom. There is little relation between the auditory and visual images in the classroom and those found in his community. He has to learn the "Look Dick, Look Jane, Run Dick, Run Jane" styles. Thus it is no small wonder that the motivation and academic achievement of Black Americans suffer. The classroom and the textbooks contain little or no talk about the Funky Chicken, The Four Corners, and other relevant aspects of the Black child's environment.

At this time I have developed a new approach to the study of ability by developing an intelligence test that is *biased* in favor of Black people. All items are taken from the culture of Black people. The name of the instrument is the "BITCH" test, which is translated "Black Intelligence Test Counterbalanced for Honkies." That is the adult form. I am also working on another test which is called "The S.O.B. Test," or the children's form. At first blush, you perhaps consider these tests as humorous. May I ask, "Is it more indicative of intelligence to know Malcolm X's last name or the author of Hamlet?" I ask you now, "When is Washington's birthday?" Perhaps 99% of you thought February 22. That answer presupposes a white norm. I actually meant Booker T. Washington's birthday, not George Washington's. "What is the color of bananas?" Many of you would say, "Yellow." But by the time the banana has made it to my community, to the ghetto, it is brown with yellow spots. So I always thought bananas were brown. Again, I was penalized by the culture in which I live. "What is the thing to do if another child hits you, without meaning to do it?" The frequency of the response is determined by the neighborhood lived in. In my community, to walk away would mean suicide. For survival purposes, children in Black communities are taught to hit back; however, that response receives zero credit on current intelligence tests such as the Stanford-Binet (Form L-M). Thus, the test items are no more relevant to the Black experience than is much of the curriculum. Black children will naturally do worse on tests which draw items from outside their culture. Conventional tests must be revalidated to include Black responses to white-oriented tests.

At the 1969 meeting of the Association of Black Psychologists in Washington, D.C., the following statement was adopted as the Association's official position:

The Association of Black Psychologists calls for a moratorium on the repeated abuse and misuse of the so-called conventional psychological tests, e.g., Stanford-Binet (Form L-M), the Wechsler, Scholastic Aptitude Test, Stanford Achievement, Iowa Basic Skills, Graduate Record Examination (GRE), the Miller Analogies Test and many others. For more than two decades, we have known that these conventional tests are unfair and improperly classify Black children. In spite of the abundance of facts, nothing has been done to correct this abuse. Thus, the Association of Black Psychologists, dedicated to preventing further exploitation of Black people, calls for an immediate moratorium on all testing of Black people until more equitable tests are available.[5]

To demonstrate further the unfairness of achievement tests, for example, in reading comprehension, I would like to check the Black comprehension level of the reader:

I was looking over this audience and I saw nothing but stone foxes. I thought to myself, as soon as the eagle flies, I'm going to go out and rent me a hog, or maybe a dence-and-a-quarter. I'm not sure. Then I want to find the H.N.I.C. of this organization to let him know that I'm going to lay dead because I'm going with my hog and stone fox to the killing floor.

Now, what did I say? The average ten-year-old Black child would do well on that reading comprehension test or one similar to the above example, but very few whites would comprehend it. It is vitally important that Black professionals articulate new approaches to the studies of Black people.

It is my contention, further, that there is a white psyche and a Black psyche, or a white life style and a Black life style. By definition, the orientation to reality of the oppressor is different from that of the oppressed. The psyche of the slave is rather different from the psyche of the master. The same is true for the victims and the victimizers. It is my contention that white psychiatrists, white psychologists, white social workers and other white mental health workers cannot successfully treat the Black psyche. These professionals may well be able to deal with that part of the Black psyche which is oriented toward becoming white and embracing middle-class values. But generally speaking it is inappropriate for the oppressor to treat the oppressed. As Eldridge so aptly remarked, "If you are not part of the solution, you're part of the problem." I add to this remark, "Since you are part of my problem, you can't be part of the solution." The wishes, hopes, and dreams of the oppressed are to replace the oppressor. I cannot see the white mental health professional comfortably dealing with the fantasy material coming out of the world of the Black psyche.

During the period 1920-1966, 9,914 doctorates were granted in psychology by 25 major universities, but only 93 of these were conferred upon Black people. Black people have not had an adequate number of Black psychologists or psychiatrists available to treat them. They have been given tranquilizing pills or electric shock treatment. We must get more Black professionals out into the community to treat the Black psyche. For example, if one of the Brothers were to visit a Black psychologist's office and comment, "I have some problems with a stone fox," I think the Black psychologist would understand the remark, but a white psychiatrist would probably say, "This patient is literal; he's concrete; he's neologistic; he's schizophrenic." The white professional who thinks like this obviously does not understand the Black patois, and has no business treating the Black mind.

Text books are loaded with the concepts of neuroses and Freudian interpretations. For the most part, Black people don't have neuroses or unreal problems. Black people have what I call "niggerosis," just from being Black, just from being called nigger, from being told we have an IQ of 82 when we recognize we are intelligent but cannot prove the fact. Niggerosis deals with real problems, like not having enough money, fighting roaches, frozen water pipes, rats, and other symptoms produced by racism. Niggerosis can't be treated by white people because they don't understand it. They don't know what it is. Frequently, I am asked: "Bob, why do you say you are a Black man first?" It is true: I am a Black man first. And the white American says, "Yes, but I'm a human." I answer, "That's right. You have been made to feel that you are human. I have been made to feel that I am a Black man, a nigger, and that is the difference, you see. The number one self-perception to me is to feel Black." Perhaps I will feel human as the conditions in America improve and develop so that I can deal with this whole issue of being human. Brother Malcolm X once commented on the American dream and becoming black in America. What is often the American dream to the white American becomes a nightmare to the Black American.

I heard someone comment recently about the mainstream of American life. Perhaps Black people shouldn't be in the mainstream of American life as it is now, because it is polluted—polluted with racism. It stinks. What I'm saying here is that we need to refocus our efforts; we need to stop studying the oppressed and start studying the oppressor. We need to examine the pathology of the oppressor, the pathology of the victimizer, the sickness of white racism. We need to understand the structure of a psyche, a life style, that forces one man to ride another's back as long as the white American has the Black.

Yes, I have a Ph.D.; I really have two Ph.D.'s: the other one is "Pool Hall Degree." I got that one early in life, and it has carried me much further in my thinking about Blackness than the other. Now I can study the mind of the oppressor to find out what makes him victimize me. What is his pathology? The pathology of whiteness? No one knows the master better than the servant.

The accusation has been made that black people in this country now are moving too fast. Henry David Thoreau once said, "If a man does not keep pace with his companions, perhaps it is because he hears a different drummer. Let him step to the music he hears, however measured or far away." I'd like to answer Thoreau with a little poem that I wrote several years ago:

SLOW DOWN BLACK MAN
Robert L. Williams, Ph.D.
(1965)

"Slow down, Black Man," you tell me,
"You're moving much too fast,
Why, at the rate you're going
You surely cannot last.

You're entitled to your rights, Son,
And you're going to get them too.
But you're rushing things too fast
And that ain't no good for you.

Sure, your demonstrations,
Your picketings, riots and such—
I know you want your rights.
But you're crowding things too much.

Notes

1. Lloyd G. Humphreys, "Racial Differences: Dilemma of College Admission," Letter to the Editor, *Science* 166 (October 10, 1969), 167.

2. Robert Williams, Letter to the Editor, *Science* 167 (January 9, 1970), 124.

3. Personal communication to the author from Professor Humphreys.

4. A. Jensen, "Input," *Psychology Today* 3 (October 1969), 4.

5. Position statement of the Association of Black Psychologists, adopted at a meeting of the Association in Washington, D. C., September 1969.

2. Educational Testing, Individual Development, and Social Responsibility

Samuel Messick and *Scarvia Anderson*

Educational and psychological tests have been harshly criticized on a number of occasions recently on the grounds that they are unfair and inadequate measures of the capabilities of particular groups of individuals—especially those from minority and poverty backgrounds and others who for a variety of reasons are educationally alienated. Robert L. Williams and the Association of Black Psychologists, for example, have called for "a moratorium on the repeated abuse and misuse of the so-called conventional psychological tests" because they "are unfair and improperly classify Black children." Indeed, they demand "an immediate moratorium on all testing of Black people until more equitable tests are available."[1] Implicit in this indictment is the premise that most educational and psychological tests are *intrinsically* biased against minority/poverty individuals and that their very use with these groups is misuse.

Responses to these charges from the testing community usually insist that the blame is misplaced—that it is not tests *per se* that are at fault but rather the recurrent misuses of tests in particular applications. What is needed, they say, is not so much the development of

Reprinted with permission from *The Counseling Psychologist* 2 (No. 2, 1970), 80-88.

more equitable tests as the elimination of unfair and inequitable testing practices.

A complicating feature of this interchange is that the reaction, although plausible and by and large correct, is not directly responsive to the charge. The charge questions the adequacy of most tests; the response admits the inadequacy of much testing practice. There are really two issues here that not only are separable but must be separated if we are to recognize that there are multiple sources of discontent and multiple courses of remedial action, each course considerably more constructive than a monolithic demand for the abolition of testing. One issue deals with the whole question of whether a test is any good—for particular types of individuals under particular circumstances—as a measure of the characteristics it purports to assess. The other issue deals with the question of test use, beginning with whether or not a test *should* be utilized for a specified purpose. The first question is a scientific one; it may be answered by appraising the test's psychometric properties, especially its construct validity. The second question is an ethical one; it must be answered by evaluating the potential consequences of the testing in terms of human values.[2] Both questions must be addressed whenever testing is considered.

In this paper we shall point out (a) that responsible standards exist for evaluating the adequacy and appropriateness of a test for a particular use and (b) that for a variety of reasons these standards are not always applied, leaving considerable room for improvement if testing is to fulfill its potential as a positive force for promoting education, training, and opportunity. We shall emphasize the various possibilities for improvement—or the many potentialities of testing—rather than the shortcomings of the present state of the field, because we feel that the indictment of testing by Williams and others must ultimately be met in terms of improved test development, application, and interpretation. Furthermore, these improvements must take into account more than the single issue of improper measurement or classification that their charge implies.

Before considering the scientific basis for evaluating whether a test measures the same thing with the same fidelity in different racial and other population groups, we will first discuss the importance, in dealing with these basic issues of bias and validity, of expanding the typically restricted definition of "test" to a more general notion of "assessment" broadly conceived. We will then turn to the problem of evaluating the appropriateness of test use in terms of the potential social consequences of the testing, underscoring the need to take into account the possibility of positive and negative side effects on both the person being tested and the person doing the testing. Finally, in view of the seriousness of the recent call for a moratorium on the testing of Black people, we will point to some of the critical social consequences of *not* testing.

Testing as Systematic Inquiry

The statements of Williams and other spokesmen for the Black community suggest that their concerns about tests are addressed almost entirely to those instruments associated with "intelligence," "IQ," and "verbal and quantitative aptitude." It is probably the case that such measures have been the ones most frequently misused, but this is partly because they have been the most frequently used. Many members of the educational establishment restrict their conception of "tests" to a similar narrow range, and this limited perspective has led both to the use of intelligence and aptitude tests in situations where they were unsuitable or unproductive and to the failure to seek and develop other means of assessing student performance, appreciation, knowledge, understanding, and judgment.

"Playing the Dozens" is a verbal jousting that depends on an imaginative derogation of the participants' backgrounds.[3] Frequently a series of episodic references are cited as the verbal interplay is intensified. It would take very little doing to turn a Dozens "game" into a test. It already has some elements of a standard stimulus (an "enemy" who is to be destroyed through attacks on his parents), a circumscribed response system (verbal, oral, in quatrains), and a scoring system (as Brown describes it, "the winner was determined by the way they responded to what you said. If you fell all over each other laughing, then you knew you'd scored.").[4] Whether or not it would be a "good" test would depend upon judgments about the importance of the content and purpose of the measurement and upon its properties in relation to other measures and performance criteria, balanced against the possible harm that such measurement might engender.

It is possible that good performance on such a test would be predictive of good performance on other verbal fluency measures and perhaps of leadership in the peer group. But it is doubtful that any educational program would take it upon itself to try to improve performance in playing the Dozens of those who earned low scores on the test.

Nevertheless, it is important to make the point that there are *many* qualities of student behavior that need to be assessed in order to identify talent and to initiate educational programs relevant to the needs of the individuals. Furthermore, these qualities can be assessed in a context that is compatible with the student's previous experiences and thus does not introduce the irrelevant difficulty of "strangeness." This strangeness or the perceived irrelevance of the test to the life experiences of the examinee represents a kind of face *in*validity, if you will, which poses a constant potential threat to the psychometric validity of the assessment in individual instances. But this strangeness is relative: its impact can be reduced by instruction and practice and, since it is not a necessary concomitant of the testing process, it may even be avoided completely by sensitive test construction and administration. For example, a second grade teacher can "test" a child's social competencies by observing him in play with his peers, his vigor in normal activities like jumping, his understanding of money through "store" exchanges, his attitudes toward members of other ethnic groups through his choice of ethnically identified playthings, his listening comprehension ability through his reaction to television messages, his manipulative skills through toy assembly projects, his interest in his school work by his eagerness to get started in the mornings, aspects of his imagination through his art work, etc. Furthermore, tasks and observations of these types can readily be standardized and even "scaled" to the extent that the teacher can order or sort the children in her class in terms of their needs for special instruction or experience.

The Adequacy of Measurement and the Question of Bias

The Association of Black Psychologists has charged that conventional tests improperly classify Black children. It is indeed true that individuals from minority and poverty backgrounds typically obtain lower scores on conventional tests than members of the White middle class, who dominate most norms groups. But it is important to inquire into the possible sources of this poorer performance, because some of the contributing factors can be counteracted. Let us consider three of these sources.

1. The Test May Measure Different Things for Different Groups

It is possible for the same test to measure different attributes or processes in minority/poverty groups than it measures in White middle-class samples or for the same processes to be captured with a different degree of fidelity. If this is the case, then scores should certainly not be interpreted in the same way in both groups, nor should performance levels in one group be compared with those in the other as if they were on the same dimension. To discount the possibility that the same instrument measures different things in different groups, it is necessary to assess the reliability and validity of the test separately for each group and to demonstrate the comparability of the obtained values. In this connection, it is particularly critical that comparability of construct validity for the different groups be appraised; this can be done by examining the patterns of correlates of the test with other measures to see if they are similar across groups. In addition, if the test is to be used for purposes of selection, classification, or guidance, its predictive validity should also be separately evaluated where technically feasible, taking care to check that there is a common criterion uniformly applied across groups.

2. The Test May Involve Irrelevant Difficulty

The estimates of the capabilities of minority/poverty groups derived from certain tests may be systematically lower than they should be because of irrelevant difficulties in the testing situation. This kind of distortion represents a bias in the measurement or estimation of ability levels in the same sense that a sample statistic which uniformly deviates from a population parameter is a biased estimate.

Some examples of irrelevant difficulty are a test format requiring a child to *read* the instructions for a task intended to assess listening comprehension ability, an answer-marking procedure that is almost as difficult as the problems posed by the test itself, and a time limit that is severely restrictive when the testing task requires varying amounts of reflection by the respondents.

Other potential sources of irrelevant difficulty include:

(a) *Items that are more germane to one group than to another.*
One way of uncovering such items is to search for response distributions that exhibit item-by-group interactions, thereby revealing items
that are relatively more difficult or relatively easier than the majority
of the items for one group as opposed to another. Items differentially favoring males or females have been uncovered over the years and
their distinctive properties elucidated,[5] but relatively few studies
have addressed themselves to the identification of items that differentially favor one racial or ethnic group over another in this sense.[6]
Whenever possible it would be a desirable addition to standard item-
analysis practice to search for such items routinely, as well as to
examine the possibility of the differential attractiveness of multiple-
choice distracters to different population groups. Such investigations
would increase our understanding of differential item properties and
of individual and group differences in item response and would provide an additional empirical basis for judging how appropriate a test
is for particular individuals and groups.

In the past, when occasional biased items were uncovered on a
test, their appearance was usually defended on the grounds of their
small contribution to total test variance or on the basis of the inclu-
sion of a sufficient number of counter-biased items to balance their
influence. These arguments addressed themselves to the problem of
biased items as threats to validity but not to the social and educational consequences of administering biased items to individuals they
are biased against.

(b) *Testing conditions that make some individuals feel anxious,
threatened, or alienated.* The adverse consequences of such negative
affects on test performance are potentially quite serious,[7] and vigor-
ous attempts should be made to prevent their occurrence, through
such steps as utilizing familiar and congenial settings and administrators, reducing the adversarial quality of the testing situation, emphasizing to the examinee the positive values of the information being
collected for educational and developmental purposes, etc.

(c) *Differences in test wiseness.* Individuals and groups differ in
their degree of test wiseness and in their familiarity with various
test-taking strategies, and this inexperience with effective approaches
to test taking may place some at a disadvantage, at least initially.
This is likely to be a more serious problem with young children than
with high school or college students. The differential effects of varia-

tions in test wiseness may be reduced by the use of clear and detailed instructions and by exposure to practice items, preferably with feedback. In addition, test-taking strategies can be taught. To the extent that such strategies of test taking are also strategies of thinking and problem solving, this effort would be generally beneficial to the student, and it would tend to increase not only the test scores but also the intrinsic validity of the test.[8] To the extent that the test-taking strategies are primarily adaptive to particular properties of the test design, the time might be better spent in improving the tests and the techniques of administering them.

3. The Test May Accurately Reflect Ability or Achievement Levels

Low scores *per se* do not necessarily indicate bias in measurement. Many of the abilities assessed by conventional tests develop out of educational, social, and family experiences over many years. Low test scores may represent an unbiased assessment of ability levels that have been limited by the cumulative impact of poverty, prejudice, inequality of educational opportunity, and other factors. The ghetto child, for example, who has attended a succession of inferior schools (with all that "inferior" implies for the quality of teachers, instruction, and facilities) and comes from a home where books and other learning supports have always been in short supply cannot be expected suddenly to handle with competency the materials and problems of the "average" curriculum—or standardized test. The bias under these conditions is not in the estimation of the ability levels but in the social forces that inhibited development. Test scores in these circumstances then become a powerful monitor of the inequities of the educational and social system, as well as a blueprint for constructive educational action at the individual level.

The Appropriateness of Test Use and the Question of Fairness

The underestimation of ability and achievement levels does not necessarily imply unfairness in the *use* of those scores. Bias in measurement and unfairness in practice are often concomitants, to be sure, but they do not have to go hand in hand. Consider a selection or placement situation where a test is valid for two groups but one group characteristically obtains lower scores than the other because of irrelevant difficulty or other sources of bias; assume also that there is not a corresponding difference in criterion performance. If the selection or placement decision is made in terms of acceptable levels of predicted criterion performance, then separate cut-off scores or regression functions would (and should) be utilized for the two groups, with an appropriately lower cut-off being employed in the low-scoring group. This is tantamount to adding points to the scores of the low-scoring group—not as a *general* strategy as described by Williams,[9] but under certain *specific* circumstances where the procedure is clearly justified; i.e., when there is external evidence of measurement bias and suffficient information to estimate the size of the effects for a particular purpose. In this example, then, we have assumed a systematic underestimation of ability levels in one group due to measurement bias and have illustrated the possibility of utilizing within-group test validity to produce a selection procedure that is not unfair to the low-scoring group.

This example dramatizes the possibility that a test might have a different validity coefficient or a different regression function for a minority/poverty group than for a middle-class group and that the general use of prediction equations derived from the White majority might unfairly penalize minority individuals in selection or placement situations. Since such an eventuality cannot be discounted on logical grounds, testing practitioners should be constantly alert to the prospect. However, investigations thus far have not produced many examples of this kind of unfairness in educational settings. On the contrary, although there may sometimes be group differences in validity coefficients and regression lines, when predictions of academic performance are based upon regression equations suitable for the *majority* group, then minority individuals are predicted to do about as well or somewhat better than they actually do.[10]

Importance and Relevance

Central to the issue of fairness in the applications of testing is the question of the appropriateness of the selected test for the proposed purpose. Judgments of whether or not a specific test should be used for a particular purpose must take into account the relevance of the attributes measured to the intended criterion and the importance of the information obtained for the given objective.[11] The appropriateness of the objective itself should also be evaluated, and this places us squarely in the arena of social values and public responsibility.

Although judgments concerning test use must be relative to specific purposes (for a test may be fine for one purpose and terrible for another), the decision should also take into account the possibility of additional consequences or side effects attendant upon the use. In addition, the potentiality for misuse must also be considered, as well as the possibility of safeguards to protect against it.

Side Effects of Testing

It should be recognized that the administration of a test may have many consequences in addition to the intended assessment. These may be either positive or negative and may affect both the examinee and the examiner.

To begin with, the taking of tests can be a rewarding enterprise and may even be fun. Our experiences in testing over a thousand Black preschoolers in the ETS Longitudinal Study of Disadvantaged Children and Their First School Experiences[12] have clearly demonstrated that this is possible. At a minimum, a test should be constructed to provide a pleasant or challenging experience for a child. At best, it would also have some instructional value in its own right. The measures developed in the ETS "Let's Look at First Graders" series,[13] for example, appear to have this property. For older students who have more understanding of what testing is about, a good test can also serve to define the objectives of a course of study, to highlight important concepts, and to stimulate the synthesis of ideas.

On the negative side, there are numerous examples of test taking as a frustrating experience for students: when the relevance of many of the items is unclear, when content is ambiguous or inaccurate, when tasks are at an inappropriate difficulty level, when—in the case of "school" tests—the test is not closely related to the student's study assignment, when there are irrelevant difficulties, when the test reinforces negative feelings the student already has toward the educational system. In addition, the context of testing can supply its own negative affect. Not many students can be expected to enjoy taking a test that may eliminate them from a competition (in contrast, for example, to one focusing less on selection and more on diagnosis for training or self-improvement).

The test administrator can also be affected by tests. If he views tests as an imposition—and many teachers do, especially when they had little voice in the decision to use them—he may not only conduct an unprofessional administration but also communicate his feelings in subtle or unsubtle ways to the examinees, with obvious consequences for their performance. Or, if he is not tuned in to the purposes of testing, he may engage in such lamentable practices as teaching the test items specifically, with little regard for the more general processes involved.

On the other hand, some testing sessions—particularly those conducted individually or in small groups as is most appropriate for younger children—provide an excellent opportunity for a teacher to observe a child intensively, to study his reactions and coping behaviors, and to identify types of situations that disturb him. These observations, made in a fairly standard situation affording comparability across many students, may provide far more valuable information than scores. In addition, a good assessment battery can do much to promote consideration of the complexity of students and the broad range of skills, attitudes, achievements, social competencies, etc., that characterize their development and underlie their responses to educational and social stimuli. A battery appropriate for use at the local level but developed nationally can also provide teachers with some protection against insularity. It can remind them of the broad goals of education and call attention to performances that other educators value.

It is important to recognize that such effects on the tested and the testers can occur relatively independently of the interpretation of results. Some of the arguments of the Black psychologists can be seen as referring to the test-taking *process* and the side effects it may have. It is the responsibility of test developers, selecters, and users, first, to recognize the possibility of such effects and, second, to edit, evaluate, and use their tests in such a way that they foster only the positive ones.

The Limits of Test Use

Most of the possible misuses of tests can be attenuated if appropriate safeguards and guiding principles are adopted in advance. In this regard, two critical problems warrant special comment; namely, the problem of misinterpretation and the problem of secondary use of test results.

1. *The problem of misinterpretation.* A large portion of the problem of poor interpretation is really a problem of poor thinking. It is

misinterpretation based upon a misconception of the phenomenon being measured or an exaggerated expectation about the infallibility of tests. One form of misconception that is particularly widespread is the presumption that test scores reflect fixed levels of capacity. Another type of frequent misinterpretation derives from the tendency to take seriously insignificant differences between scores. The former error can only be overcome by training and enlightenment, but the latter error of overinterpreting small differences can be substantially reduced by judicious presentation of results—through the use of percentile bands, stanine scores, quartiles, or other devices. In general, a number of kinds of misinterpretation can be avoided by careful presentation of scores, and one important guiding principle is that the presentation should relate as directly as possible to the types of decisions to be made on the basis of the results.

2. *The problem of secondary use.* The secondary use of test results raises a key issue in the ethics of testing. When, if ever, is it appropriate to use test results collected at one point in time for one purpose at another point in time for either the same or a different purpose? Suppose someone wanted to use third-grade test scores in counseling eleventh graders about their chances of success on a college admissions test. Or information from a biographical inventory collected to determine a school district's eligibility for Title I funds to place students in remedial classes. Or ninth-grade biology scores to support a recommendation about a student's eligibility for advanced placement in biology. Or test data from the 1947 freshman class to write a paper on how freshmen have changed in the last quarter century.

The decision on secondary use must face the same two requirements as the decision on primary use—the need to justify the proposed procedure on scientific grounds and in terms of its potential social consequences. In terms of scientific criteria alone, such actions as those just described might be justified if it could be shown empirically that the test results were indeed valid predictors of performance at another point in time or in another arena—or, in the case of the last example above, that the design of the analysis and the measurement properties of the instruments allowed valid comparisons.

But the ethical question of "*Should* these actions be taken?" cannot be answered by a simple appeal to empirical validity alone. The various social consequences of these actions must be contended with, especially those bearing on issues of invasion of privacy, confidentiality of records, and client welfare. As might be expected from the diversity of potential secondary uses illustrated above, there is no single principle or set of principles that can appropriately be applied to all situations, types of measurement, or population groups. Value judgments have to be made about each, taking into account local attitudes and personnel involved as well as more general scientific and humanistic concerns.

The conflict between advancement of science and the general social welfare on the one hand and protection of the rights and privacy of individuals on the other is especially salient when test results are proposed for some use other than that originally intended. For example, the decision of a few years ago to remove all ethnic identification from student and other personnel records was viewed by most laymen as a guarantee of civil rights but by many social scientists as an unfortunate and needless constraint, for it prohibited them in many instances from developing some of the very information that government and educational agencies and representatives of minority groups are now clamoring for—information that would enable better placement of minority group members in training programs and jobs or would throw light on possible discriminatory practices.

The Social Consequences of *Not* Testing

In spite of imperfections in current tests and testing practices, it is clear that educational and psychological tests serve many critical functions—not always optimally, to be sure, but better than proposed alternatives. As we face the recent call by the Association of Black Psychologists for an immediate moratorium on all testing of Black people, we must pause to ponder what might be lost by the elimination of testing.

To begin with, the needs that testing serves would still exist and would be addressed by other means. If objective and standardized tests were not available, people would revert to the uses of the past—to subjective appraisals such as the interview and inquiries into ancestry. And one consequence of this seems clear—the likelihood of bias and discrimination would increase. A recent study[14] has shown, for example, that minority group members are rated systematically lower on pre-employment interview dimensions in the absence of interviewer knowledge of test scores, as compared with the level of interview ratings obtained for comparable groups when interviewers have such knowledge. Other research[15] indicates that supervisor's ratings vary as a function of the race of the rater and the race of the ratee, as does the validity of predicting such ratings as criteria of job performance.

In addition, without tests in educational and job-training programs, teachers and counselors would be forced to rely only upon observations of skills and deficiencies during the course of the program. Although this might in many instances provide important information upon which to base subsequent treatment, it would also require a prolonged period of time to collect and would rarely be done systematically. Practitioners would thus be faced with the prospect of slow assessment, whereby valuable educational time must be diverted to preliminary observation before specialized treatment can be sensibly applied.

The elimination of tests would also mean the loss of one of the best ways for teachers to acquire a useful appreciation of the broad range of competencies and traits that characterize human behavior or to develop needed sensitivities to the nuances of cognitive growth. An increased parochialism might spread throughout education because of the absence of a national normative perspective and the limitation of access to concrete examples of what other educators deem important to assess. And of utmost importance, there would be an absence of yardsticks for gauging the effectiveness of educational programs and for evaluating the equity of the educational system.

Thus, the social consequences of *not* testing are extreme. Tests may be eliminated only at a cost, and a large portion of that cost would be increases in discrimination and ignorance.

Notes

1. R. L. Williams, "Black Pride, Academic Relevance, and Individual Achievement," *The Counseling Psychologist* 2 (No. 1, 1970), 18-22.

2. S. Messick, "Personality Measurement and the Ethics of Assessment," *American Psychologist* 20 (February 1965), 136-42; D. N. Jackson and S. Messick, "The Ethics of Assessment," in D. N. Jackson and S. Messick (eds.), *Problems in Human Assessment* (New York: McGraw-Hill, Inc., 1967).

3. Williams, *op. cit.*

4. H. R. Brown, *Die, Nigger, Die!* (New York: The Dial Press, Inc., 1969).

5. W. E. Coffman, "Sex Differences in Response to Items in an Aptitude Test," in *Eighteenth Yearbook* of the National Council on Measurement in

Education (Ames, Iowa: National Council on Measurement in Education, 1961), 117-24.

6. T. A. Cleary and T. L. Hilton, "An Investigation of Item Bias," *Educational and Psychological Measurement* 28 (Spring 1968), 61-75.

7. Irwin Katz, "Experimental Studies of Negro-White Relationships," in L. Berkowitz (ed), *Advances in Experimental Social Psychology* 5 (New York: Academic Press, 1970), 71-117.

8. H. Gulliksen, "Intrinsic Validity," *American Psychologist* 5 (October 1950), 511-17.

9. R. L. Williams, "From Dehumanization to Black Intellectual Genocide: A Rejoinder," *Clinical Child Psychology Newsletter* 9 (Fall 1970), 6-7.

10. T. A. Cleary, "Test Bias: Prediction of Grades of Negro and White Students in Integrated Colleges," *Journal of Educational Measurement* 5 (Summer 1968), 115-24: S. A. Kendrick and C. L. Thomas, "Transition From School to College," *Review of Educational Research* 40 (February 1970), 151-79; J. C. Stanley and A. C. Porter, "Correlation of Scholastic Aptitude Test Scores with College Grades for Negroes versus Whites," *Journal of Educational Measurement* 4 (Winter 1967), 199-218; G. Temp, "An Examination of Test Bias: Some Data, Some Questions," *Research Bulletin*, Educational Testing Service (1970).

11. American Psychological Association Task Force on Employment Testing of Minority Groups, "Job Testing and the Disadvantaged," *American Psychologist* 24 (July 1969), 637-50; American Psychological Association, "Psychological Assessment and Public Policy," *American Psychologist* 25 (March 1970), 264-66.

12. S. B. Anderson, "From Textbooks to Reality: Social Researchers Face the Facts of Life in the World of the Disadvantaged," in Jerome Hellmuth (ed.) *Disadvantaged Child*, Vol. 3, *Compensatory Education: A National Debate* (New York: Brunner/Mazel Publishers, 1970), 226-37.

13. *Let's Look at Children* (Princeton, N. J.: Educational Testing Service, 1965).

14. C. P. Sparks and W. R. Manese, "Interview Ratings with and without Knowledge of Pre-employment Test Scores," *The Experimental Publication System* (1970), 1-10.

15. R. L. Flaugher, J. T. Campbell, and L. W. Pike, "Prediction of Job Performance for Negro and White Medical Technicians," *Project Report 69-5* (Princeton, N. J.: Educational Testing Service, 1969).

3. Concepts of Culture-Fairness

Robert L. Thorndike

Fairness of a test relates to fair use. One definition of fair use states that a common qualifying score may be used with two groups if the regression line based on one group does not systematically over- or under-predict criterion performance in the other. However, it is shown that when the two groups differ appreciably in mean test score, the above procedure, which is "fair" to individual members of the group scoring lower on the test, is "unfair" to the lower group as a whole in the sense that the proportion qualified on the test will be smaller, relative to the higher-scoring group, than the proportion that will reach any specified level of criterion performance. An alternate definition would specify that the qualifying scores on a test should be set at levels that will qualify applicants in the two groups in proportion to the fraction of the two groups reaching a specified level of criterion performance.

Over the past several years, there has been a gradual increase in concern about "culture-fairness" of tests and testing procedures. The problems that are involved are partly problems of empirical fact, but partly problems of definition. Thus, on the one hand, Cleary

Reprinted with permission from the *Journal of Educational Measurement* 8 (Summer 1971), 63-70, published by the National Council on Measurement in Education.

found in several integrated colleges that the regression equation for predicting college achievement from SAT score based on white students was appropriate for black students.[1] But this result can only be accepted as evidence of culture-fairness if one also accepts Cleary's definition that a test is culture-fair for populations A and B when the regression equation based on population A neither systematically over- nor under-predicts level of performance for members of population B. However, this is only one possible definition.

One type of definition insists that a test is fair only if there is no difference in mean score between populations A and B, and that wherever a difference is found it is evidence of test bias. However, it hardly seems useful to equate fairness with identity. This type of definition prejudges the reality of differences between groups, ruling them out *a priori.*

If one acknowledges that differences in average test performance may exist between populations A and B, then a judgment on test-fairness must rest on the inferences that are made from the test rather than on a comparison of mean scores in the two populations. One must then focus attention on fair *use* of the test scores, rather than on the scores themselves. Since there are many different uses that can be made of a particular test or inferences that can be based upon it, it is entirely possible that one use or inference is fair while another is grossly unfair. By way of illustration, the test item

The usual temperature for baking a cake is about
(A) 250°   (B) 300°   (C) 350°   (D) 400°

would probably favor females over males so far as the percent of right answers is concerned, and so might be considered "unfair" to males. However, if the criterion being predicted by the item is how palatable a cake one can make, the poorer performance of males on the item may well be paralleled by comparably poorer performance in the kitchen. On the other hand, if scores on this item were used to estimate "range of general information," one might well object to it as biased against and unfair to males. It is in this sense that we should speak not of a fair or unfair (biased) test, but of fair or unfair test use.

The presence (or absence) of differences in mean score between groups, or of differences in variability, tells us nothing directly about fairness of test use. Admittedly, we are more likely to raise the issue when there *are* differences. But differences in score distributions do not, *per se,* constitute evidence of unfairness. One must examine the correlates of those differences. In fact, one must examine *each* correlate, and determine to what extent inferences with respect to *that* correlate can be made for the group in question using the test in question, and how those inferences should be made.

When we speak of correlates, this implies that there is some significant relationship between the test and the thing with which it is being correlated. If there is *no* relationship, there is then no basis for inference of any kind (fair or unfair) from the test and consequently our objection should be not that the test is *unfair,* but that it is *irrelevant.* There is no justification for making inferences from, and consequently for using such a test for such a purpose in any group. This state of affairs is a possibility that we cannot ignore when tests are used in personnel selection or even for educational placement decisions.

Given that a significant relationship exists in group A, the issue of "fairness" centers around a comparison of the relationship in group A and in group B. We can picture the relationship between test and correlated variable (which we shall from now on speak of as the *criterion* variable) by a bivariate scatter of scores, somewhat as shown in Figure 1. Figure 1 is drawn to represent a bivariate distribution with equal standard deviations for the two variables and a correlation of 0.50 between them.

In Figure 3-1, the more horizontal line shows the regression of criterion measure on test score. At each test score level, this line goes through the average criterion score and consequently the predicted criterion score for that test performance. In our illustration, it is the line $y = r_{xy} x$, or $y = 0.50x$.* The more nearly vertical line shows the other regression—the regression of test score on criterion. It is the average test score for persons having a given criterion score. Generally, this second regression is not of practical value, though it may be of theoretical interest in some contexts.

When we have a special group of some sort that is identifiably different from the general group with which we started out, we may examine the scatter-plots of the two groups to see in what respects they are the same and in what respects they differ. They may differ

---

*In the interest of simplicity of presentation, the regression has been expressed in terms of deviations from the major group mean.

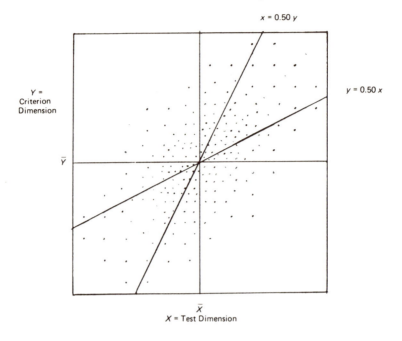

Figure 3-1. Regression lines for criterion and test

in mean score on either the test or the criterion variable or both, in variability on either test or criterion or both, and/or in slope of the lines of regression. If there is no difference in any of these respects, then, obviously, there is no issue concerning fairness of the test in relation to that criterion. Concern about fairness usually arises when the mean test score of some special group (called here the minor group) is noticeably lower than the mean of the major group of the population.

Let us consider first the relatively simple condition in which the slope of the regression line is the same for both groups, and the minor group differs from the major group only in its mean score on the test (X), the criterion measure (Y), or more typically both. Several illustrative examples of such differences are shown in Figure 3-2.

In Figure 3-2, it has been assumed that the minor group's mean test score falls exactly one standard deviation below that of the major group. It is further assumed that a criterion score is available for all members of each group. This implies that all members had been

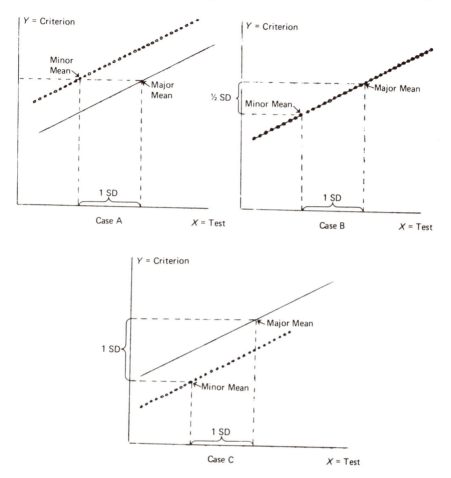

Figure 3-2. Regressions with common slope for major
and minor group

admitted to the educational program, training program, or job, without regard to their score on the test. Remember that at this point it
has been assumed that the slopes of the regression of criterion on test
score are the same within both groups.

Figure 3-2 displays three model situations: Case A, in which the two
groups have the same average criterion score; Case B, in which the
minor group has a mean criterion score falling one half standard
deviation below that for the major group and consequently falling on

the major group regression line $y = 0.50x$ for predicting criterion from test; and Case C, in which the minor group falls the same distance below the major group on the criterion as on the test, to wit, one full standard deviation. For each of Cases A and C, the regression line of criterion on test for the minor group is shown as a separate line of circles; for Case B this line coincides with the regression line for the major group.

Case A is one in which the test is obviously "unfair" to the minor group. Here, a group whose average criterion score equals that of the major group falls far below it on the predictor test. This case would be exemplified if it were found that, given certain conditions of adaptive and remedial instruction, a group of culturally deprived youngsters with mean IQ of 85 could be brought to the same level of proficiency in a clerical position that was displayed by an unselected sample with an IQ of 100. In Case A, the regression line for the minor group falls clearly *above* that for the major group, and individuals in the minor group at a specific test score level perform better on the criterion, on average, than those in the major group at the same score level.

Case B is one in which the regression lines of criterion on test score for the two groups coincide. Thus, for any given test score, the predicted criterion score for an individual is the same without regard to the group of which he is a member. This might seem to be a reasonable definition of "fairness," and by this definition Case B represents an instance in which inference of criterion performance from the test score is scrupulously "fair." This is the interpretation that Cleary[2] makes, and it is the one that would often be made by psychologists concerned with educational or industrial testing.

Note, however, that in Case B the minor group differs from the major group by only half a standard deviation on the criterion variable, while differing by a full standard deviation on the test. The overlapping of the two groups is much greater for the criterion measure than for the test score. For example, making one or two simple assumptions,* we come to the conclusion that about 16% of the minor group would come up to the major group average on the test while about 31% would come up to the major group average on the criterion measure. If this value (the major group average) were set as

*A normal distribution and a standard deviation equal to that of the major group on both test and criterion measure.

a requirement for admission, the test would qualify only 16% of the minor group versus 50% of the major, whereas in the total minor group 31% would reach the critical level on the criterion measure defined by the median of the major group. The percents would be different, of course, if other critical levels in the major group were selected as representing adequate criterion performance, but the basic relationship would remain. A larger percentage of the total minor group would achieve the acceptable criterion level than would be accepted on the basis of the test.

What appears to be happening here is that the test is measuring some factors that are common to it and the criterion variable and (since the correlation is less than perfect) some factors that are *not* shared between test and criterion. Since the mean scores of the two groups differ more on the test than on the criterion, whatever factors are unique to the test differentiate the two groups much more sharply than the factors that are unique to the criterion. Thus, though the test is fair in relation to the *shared* variance, it is unfair with respect to the variance that is unique to test or criterion, one or both.

A specific example that would produce the two means of Case B would be one in which the loading of a common factor was 0.71 for both test and criterion, and consequently the loading of a specific factor for each was also 0.71. [Note that $(0.71)^2 + (0.71)^2 = 1.00$.] Equations that would produce a mean of -1.00 S.D. on the test and of -0.50 S.D. on the criterion are:

$$
\begin{array}{cc}
\text{General} & \text{Specific} \\
\text{Factor} & \text{Factor} \\
\overline{X}_{\text{Minor}} = 0.71\,(-0.71) + 0.71\,(-0.71) = -1.00 \\
\overline{Y}_{\text{Minor}} = 0.71\,(-0.71) + 0.71\,(0.00) \quad = -0.50
\end{array}
$$

Thus, members of the minor group are here being penalized because they are being treated as if they fall as far below the major group on the unique portion of the criterion as they do on the unique part of the test, and this is not the case. In this illustration, the minor group is shown as falling 0.71 standard deviations below the major group on the factor common to test and criterion, the same distance below on the factor specific to the test, and exactly at the major group mean on the factor specific to the criterion. Of course, there are many other ways in which the same mean scores could be produced. It seems that we are forced to conclude that in Case B though the test may be fair to minor group members as individuals, the test is still "unfair" to the minor group as a group.

We may now turn our attention to Case C. Here, the minor group differs as much from the major group on the criterion as it does on the predictor test. Under these circumstances, the two groups differ as much with respect to the factors that are unique to the test as they do with respect to the factors that are unique to the criterion. The test is "fair" with respect to its unique nonvalid variance, as well as with respect to its valid variance. If we were to use any specified critical test score and apply it to both groups, a smaller percentage of the minor group than of the major group would be accepted, but this smaller percentage would in this case exactly parallel the smaller percentage reaching a specified level of performance on the criterion measure.

Note, however, that the regression line of the minor group for predicting the criterion falls well below that for the major group. At a given test score level, average criterion performance is lower for a minor group member than for a major group member. Group membership is itself a datum that has some significance for criterion performance over and above the information provided by the test, since the groups differ with respect to the variance that is unique to the criterion and is not measured by the test.

In Case C, the discrepancy of the minor group is of the same size (in standard deviation units) on the criterion as it is on the test. Thus, we could expect substantially the same proportion on test and criterion to reach any specified percentile level defined with respect to the major group. It should be noted, however, that in this case, as in the others, an acceptance procedure that bases the proportion of minor group members accepted on the fraction of prior samples from that group achieving a specified criterion score will almost universally accept *individuals* who do less well on the criterion, on average, than individuals from the major group. This will be true *whenever* the minor group test mean falls below the major group test mean and the correlation between test and criterion is less than perfect. Under these conditions, the two definitions of fairness—one based on predicted criterion score for individuals and the other on the distribution of criterion scores in the two groups—will always be in conflict. The extent of their discrepancy will increase in direct proportion to the difference between the major and minor group test means and will be inversely related to the correlation between test and criterion score.

If one defines "fair" use of a test, as we have done in our discussion of Case C, as providing each group the same opportunity for admission to training or to a job as would be represented by the proportion of the group falling above a specified criterion score on the correlated variable of training or job performance, then it does not matter particularly if the slope of the regression of criterion on test differs in the two groups. Having set a standard for the major group, one independently sets a critical score that will admit the required percent from the minor group (i.e., the percentage of the group that have been found to achieve the specified criterion score). So long as the test continues to have *some* validity for the criterion, one should pick the individuals having the highest test scores as being the ones with the best prospects for success on the criterion.

If one accepts the more conventional, but perhaps less defensible, definition of "fair" use of a test that is based on predicted criterion performance, one would set some level or standard of predicted criterion performance as the requirement for acceptance, and would apply this standard to both major and minor groups. For each group one would use the regression equation previously established for that group. One would define the critical test score for each group as the score that corresponded to a specified probability (perhaps 50%) of achieving the minimum acceptable criterion score.

Figure 3-3 shows an example in which the slopes of the two regressions differ fairly markedly. The figure illustrates three levels of criterion performance as required for acceptance. At the lowest, a lower score would be accepted in the minor than in the major group. At the intermediate level, a slightly higher score would be required in the minor group. At the highest qualifying level, the qualifying score would be substantially higher in the minor group. The difference arises from the fact that the regression line of the minor group in the illustration has a much flatter slope than that of the major group. Thus, the way in which a test can be used "fairly" for an individual depends on the standard of job proficiency that is chosen as representing acceptable performance.

The discussion of "fairness" in what has gone before is clearly oversimplified. In particular, it has been based upon the premise that the available criterion score is a perfectly relevant, reliable and

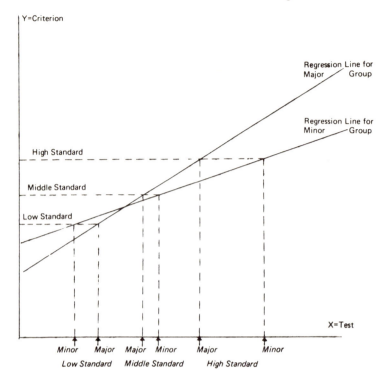

Figure 3-3. Regressions with different slope in major
and minor groups

unbiased measure of competence in the "job" (including educational
or training programs) for which candidates are being selected. The
criterion measure always falls short on at least two, if not all three,
of the above counts. It certainly falls short of perfect relevance and
reliability, and it may be biased.

If the criterion measure is itself biased in an unknown direction
and degree, no rational procedure can be set up for "fair" use of the
test. To determine what test scores in the two groups predict a given
criterion rating is fruitless if the criterion rating does not really mean
the same thing in the major and minor groups. And by the same
token, setting up group quotas based on proportions in previous
major and minor groups that have achieved a specified criterion rating is fruitless if the criterion rating signifies different things in the
two groups.

If the criterion measure is unreliable, and if one can obtain some reasonable estimate of its reliability, one can make a plausible estimate of the "true score" overlap of the criterion distribution for the two groups. Thus, the standard deviation of "criterion estimated true scores" will be $\sigma_c\sqrt{1 - r_{cc'}}$, where σ_c is the standard deviation of obtained scores on the criterion and r_{cc} is the reliability coefficient for the criterion. Thus, if the minor group mean falls 0.70 standard deviation units below the major group mean on the observed criterion score and if the reliability of the criterion score in the major group is 0.51 (a realistic, and sometimes an optimistic, estimate for criterion measures), then the standard deviation of estimated "true" criterion scores will be only $\sqrt{1 - .51}$, or 0.7 times as great as that for observed scores. Since the mean of the minor group may be considered an unbiased estimate of its true value, in "estimated true score units" of the major group the difference between the two groups is $0.7 \div 0.7 = 1.0$. The estimate of proportion of the minor group truly achieving as well on the job as any specified fraction of the major group should be based on this difference between the groups on "estimated true criterion performance."

When the criterion measure is only partially relevant (as is always the case)—that is, when it measures only certain aspects of job performance and also measures some things that are unrelated to job performance—a large question mark is introduced into any plan for fair use of a test. Since one cannot know whether the variance that is missing from the criterion measure, together with the variance that is inappropriately in it, would favor or more seriously handicap a minor group, it becomes impossible to be sure what adjustment in critical score, if any, is appropriate for minor group members. This is true whichever of the interpretations of "fairness" is guiding one's choice.

Notes

1. T. A. Cleary, "Test Bias: Prediction of Grades of Negro and White Students in Integrated Colleges," *Journal of Educational Measurement* 5 (Summer 1968), 115-24.
2. *Ibid.*

Part Two
Using Tests in Selecting Students
for Educational Opportunities

Critical issues about college entrance testing have arisen not because scholastic aptitude tests have failed to indicate students likely to earn good grades in college but because they have not served well the educational needs and aspirations of students who vary in significant respects from the traditional academically successful students. Scholastic aptitude tests are built by a procedure that seeks to maximize the correlation between the test score and the grades he receives in college. The kinds of test exercises that are included are those measuring primarily verbal facility, knowledge of quantitative relations, and computational skills. By selecting those items that discriminate most sharply between students receiving high grades in college and those given low ones, candidates who are not likely to succeed without changes in educational practices receive low scores, and in selective admissions programs would not be admitted to colleges. Thus, college staffs do not encounter many students who do not survive typical teaching practices. Hence, college instructors are not stimulated to discover and design procedures that will help such students learn. Furthermore, the term "scholastic aptitude" implies to the college instructor that students with low scores don't have the ability to succeed in college. In this way, these tests become self-fulfilling prophecies. High school grade point averages and rank in class are also measures of the student's success in getting along in the traditional system and not comprehensive assessments of what he can learn.

As the College Board Commission points out, if college practices are to be broadened to help a wider range of students get an education, so-called "aptitude testing" must become a device for assessing and reporting the variety of talents, interests, positive attitudes, and successful experiences that characterize the high school graduate. In effect, aptitude testing should seek to furnish a comprehensive inventory of the strengths and limitations, interests and goals of each person. With this information, the post-high school institution can make a much wiser selection of students for that institution; and the faculty is provided with information much more helpful in designing the curriculum and working out the teaching-learning procedures than information limited to the student's previous scholastic success and scores on tests designed to predict his grades in a traditional setting. With a student who has not found significant and relevant experience in school, information about his out-of-school accomplishments in work, in community enterprises, in peer-group activities, and in the home are more likely to indicate strengths on which his educational program can be based than the data furnished by SAT scores or high school grades.

This chapter contains three excerpts from a significant report published in 1970 by the College Entrance Examination Board. In January, 1967, the Board appointed a Commission on Tests chaired by David Tiedeman and including nineteen other leading educators. The Commission was asked to "undertake a thorough and critical review of the Board's testing function in American education and to consider possibilities for fundamental changes in the present tests and their uses in schools, colleges, and universities." After three years of work the Commission prepared a comprehensive report. The three selections from this report reproduced here serve admirably to highlight the problems and issues involved in using current tests as a primary basis for selecting students for college admission.

The first of the excerpts deals with the importance of college entrance testing and calls for a recognition of important matters to be considered if such testing is to serve the interests of the youth who take the tests, the institutions they attend, and society at large.

The second excerpt comes from a section of the report in which the functions of college board tests are listed and some major criticisms of the tests are discussed. This excerpt deals with what the report termed a "more serious criticism of the tests."

The final excerpt is a "Brief" submitted by Edmund Gordon, a member of the Commission. Gordon presents clearly the need to improve testing so as to identify a wider range of talents among college applicants and to encourage college teachers and personnel officers to develop educational procedures appropriate for students from diverse backgrounds and with varying abilities.

4. The Importance of College Entrance Testing

Commission on Tests
College Entrance Examination Board

College entrance testing such as that offered by the Board is extremely important today. Ultimately the Board's tests' importance derives not from the fact that about 1,000 colleges require them and about 2,000,000 students take them each year, but rather from the fact that going to college has come to seem so important. Earlier in this century the Board's tests—or any other agency's—could have been taken by all college freshmen and still not have been as important as those taken by two-thirds of them today. Such tests are so important today because going to college is so important today.

Throughout this century about half of the nation's high school graduates have gone to college; since about 1960 this fraction has been increasing. However, from 1880 until 1950 or 1960 the incidence of college-going among high school graduates was constant except for fluctuations during the Depression and the World Wars: about half of all white male high school graduates went to college and about 4 in 10 of all white female high school graduates and of all nonwhite graduates of both sexes went to college.[1] But there were,

College Entrance Examination Board, *Righting the Balance*, Report of the Commission on Tests, Vol. 1 (New York: College Entrance Examination Board, 1970), 28-32. Reproduced by permission.

proportionately, so few high school graduates earlier in the century that it didn't make much difference to very many people where half of them went to college or what tests they had to take to do so.

As the incidence of high school graduation has grown, so has the incidence of college-going and attendant external college entrance tests, of college graduation, and of graduate or professional school entry. If these trends continue, by about 1980 only 1 young American in 10 will not graduate from high school; well over half—6, perhaps 7—of the other nine will go immediately to college; and virtually all of this college entry will be mediated in part by tests, much of it by tests of the College Entrance Examination Board. Several factors, including geography, sex, social class, race, and high school record have much more to do with who goes where to college than do college entrance tests, of which the SAT [Scholastic Aptitude Test] is only one. The importance of the SAT in the admissions process probably varies from college to college, and the College Board does not intend that it should be as important as it appears to be for some admissions officers. However, all these determinants are interconnected, and the College Board's program of tests, if not the most important of them, is certainly one of the most salient. The tests are therefore a sort of lightning rod, which results in their drawing both useful criticism and criticism that could with more effect be directed elsewhere, but which also results in their being a convenient focus for discussion of the entire college entrance process and its implications for education generally and for society at large.

Statistics of growth such as those noted above for the rates of high school graduation and college entry are usually delivered in a tone of approval in America, especially if they reflect, as these seem to at least superficially, an increase in educational attainment. However, it is not at all obvious that these trends, together or severally, are entirely desirable. To establish that would require a close look at what lies behind these statistics, and at what lies outside them, to see what are the social consequences of institutionalizing education for so long for so many.

One thing is clear: modern economy and modern society being what they are in the United States, anything—including obviously tests—that mediates college entry helps to determine in the process who will eventually get in which graduate schools, who will eventually (or immediately in the case of those who do not go to graduate schools) get which or no jobs, who meets and eventually marries whom, and so forth. To state it so, and to assert simultaneously that increasingly going to college seems to be the only way to "make it" in America today, implies the obvious: whether or where given students go to college must be a matter of great personal concern to both those students and to their parents.

But this is more than a matter of personal concern, because the mediating factors, including tests, also help to determine what *kinds* of students will eventually get into what *kinds* of graduate schools and will eventually get what *kinds* of jobs, and so on. That is, more status is attached to certain educational patterns than to others and to certain occupational and social roles than to others, and the former—to which people are distributed partly by test scores—are passports to the latter. But the process is apparently circular, because social, including racial, characteristics are related to the distribution of test scores: on the average, white children score higher than non-white children; middle-class children score higher than lower-class children, and so forth.

This existing process must be squared with the earlier assertion that the increasing use of the SAT and objective Achievement Tests had helped some prestigious and formerly socially exclusive colleges democratize their student bodies. More precisely, they helped those colleges make their services accessible—via competition based partly on scholastic aptitude—largely to all the middle class, which of course includes most Americans, whereas they had formerly been restricted largely to the professional and managerial classes whose members could afford, and were disposed, to enroll their children in secondary schools teaching the previously required curriculum.

It is difficult to estimate precisely how much the SAT and similar tests have had or still have to do with providing social mobility via higher education; certainly their increasing use coincides with the increase in the socioeconomic diversity of selective colleges' student bodies. Strictly on the basis of SAT scores, however, the more socially advantaged students would tend to be accepted over the less so because their test scores tend to be higher; similarly whites would tend to be accepted over nonwhites, other than orientals. For example, if all (and only) the high school seniors who scored above the current national average (about 375) on the verbal sections of the SAT went to college, then nearly half of the white seniors of both sexes would go but only perhaps 15 percent of the black seniors would.[2] Thus a strict selection on the basis of scholastic aptitude, which is largely a matter of verbal ability, would promote some young people from modest circumstances and a few from America's "underclass" over more advantaged youth and would make the rate of college entrance for young women equal to that for young men. But rather than removing class and racial biases from American higher education it would reinforce them.

Considerations such as these make it clear that the tests and associated services intervening between high school and college, especially those of the College Board that touch directly as they do the lives of over a quarter of the nation's young people, are a matter of some importance, not just to the Board, those young people, and the institutions they attend, but also to society at large. So large and pervasive an enterprise should, as should the educational system it supports, be managed in the public interest. The challenge for the College Board is to discern that interest and effectively serve it.

Notes

1. A. J. Jaffe and Walter Adams, "Trends in College Enrollment," *College Board Review,* No. 55 (Winter 1964-65), 27-32.

2. S. A. Kendrick, "The Coming Segregation of Our Selective Colleges," *College Board Review,* No. 66 (Winter 1967-68), 6-13.

5. Functions and Criticisms of College Board Tests

Commission on Tests
College Entrance Examination Board

A more serious criticism of the tests the Board currently offers in the Admissions Testing Program is that in performing their current selective or distributive function they have corrupted the process of education itself. This is said to happen in various ways. One is by constricting the curriculum of secondary schools by offering curriculum-specific tests such as the Achievement Tests for which students must be prepared if they are not to be disadvantaged in the competition for college entrance.[1] College entrance tests have been liable to this charge since the secondary schools became comprehensive and assumed responsibilities other than preparing students for college entry. The response of the College Board has been to make its Achievement Tests less and less specific to any particular curriculum in a given subject. This response coincided with the interest of the professors and teachers on examining committees and in colleges and schools of measuring the students' mental prowess within a given subject more than their knowledge of discrete facts. The result is that the College Board's Achievement Tests have become more like aptitude tests.

College Entrance Examination Board, *Righting the Balance,* Report of the Commission on Tests, Vol. 1 (New York: College Entrance Examination Board, 1970), 44-48. Reproduced by permission.

There are of course many modes in which mental prowess can be expressed even within a particular subject. Curriculum study and development groups often feel that the Board's tests retard the adoption of their innovations and that they would be a good vehicle for spreading them if they could be "tipped" toward their view of their subject. The Board has tried to take a middle ground, but, in taking it, has been exposed to criticism both for incorporating innovations too quickly, and thereby dictating the course of development to the schools, and for retarding that development.

To complicate the situation further, the Achievement Tests have always served a dual function of providing information significant both for "selective" admissions at the institutional level and for distribution to courses or placement below it. The more "selective" colleges are taking students with scores toward the top of the SAT score scale. The SAT retains its predictive validity throughout its entire scale, but the Achievement Tests help to discriminate among students at the very top of it.[2] But some Achievement Tests are also useful for placement in college courses after admission,[3] despite the fact that they are not designed for that purpose and are geared instead to secondary school curriculums, which are not very well articulated with college curriculums. And here another criticism of the Achievement Tests enters; the need now is not for increasingly fine distinctions between the most apt of students, but rather for sensitive placement devices to help colleges successfully instruct all students now going to college.[4] Although the Board is sensitive to that need, it has not yet found a way to have the Achievement Tests both bolster "selective" admissions and at the same time serve satisfactorily the placement function for a broader group of students.

Neither has the Commission, which feels that fine discriminations at the top of the aptitude scale are not a pressing problem and which attaches much more importance to the problem of supporting all students—in effect the full cohort of American youth as well as many adults—in finding their way to appropriate programs of postsecondary education. And the Commission does believe it is possible to provide information services appropriate for all students, schools, and colleges, without unduly restricting the schools' curriculums.

There is however another sense in which tests are liable to criticism on the grounds that they restrict the curriculum and modes of instruction, and at the collegiate as well as at the secondary level. This criticism has been pressed by members of the Commission. In essence, it is that tests and their associated services, by accurately identifying those students who will normally "do well" in college in the "natural" course of things, thereby support those colleges in an educationally and socially dysfunctional policy of seeking and enrolling only those students who are likely to make good grades in the standard curriculums as they are usually taught.

Thus highly selective colleges reject students whose particular configuration of talents does not make them easy to instruct successfully by classic methods in traditional subjects, and less selective colleges emulate them insofar as they are able. As a result virtually the entire collection of colleges offers programs, and instruction for them, that are apparently completed by less than half of the college-going population. The other students are pushed from the system after enrollment in institutions and programs where admission is "open."

In the view then of some members of the Commission, current tests and their associated services corrupt the process of education by stultifying its development and also have the unfortunate effect of providing a rationale for its nondevelopment, since it can always be said of the unsuccessful students that they don't have what it takes—that they are not "college material."

Notes

1. Robert I. Sperber, superintendent of schools, Brookline, Massachusetts, pointed out to the Commission that not only is the curriculum constricted, but even where innovative courses are available individual students may avoid them for fear of making lower test scores.

2. Dean K. Whitla, director, Office of Tests, Harvard University, told the Commission that at Harvard College the Achievement Tests provide more useful information on applicants than does the SAT. Readers are reminded, however— as was the Commission by Julian C. Stanley, professor of education at The Johns Hopkins University and Chairman of the Board's Committee of Examiners in Aptitude Testing, of which Mr. Whitla is also a member—that selective colleges such as Harvard realize many of the predictive advantages of the SAT by students selecting or de-selecting themselves on the basis of their PSAT or SAT scores.

3. Scott Elledge, professor of English, Cornell University and chairman of the Board's Panel of Examiners in English, for example, told the Commission that the English Composition Test was superior to the Advanced Placement Examination in English as a placement device. Micheline Dufau, associate professor of French, University of Massachusetts, and chairman of the Board's Commission of Examiners for the French Listening Test, testified that the foreign language

tests are useful for placement purposes. J. Alfred Southworth, director of guidance, University of Massachusetts, concurred in his testimony with Miss Dufau's judgment while criticizing the fact that the tests' costs had doubled in the last five years.

4. Richard R. Perry, director of admissions and records, The University of Toledo, made this point most forcefully and endorsed the suggestion of Sister Jacinta Mann, director of admissions, Seton Hall College, that a series of less difficult advanced placement examinations might be very useful.

6. Toward a Qualitative Approach to Assessment

Edmund W. Gordon

Much of the impetus for the development of a technology of assessment related to intellective function and achievement resulted from and has been maintained by a supply-and-demand approach to access to education and distribution of educational opportunities. Access to a limited supply of educational opportunities has been guarded by selection procedures that, prior to the twentieth century, were based on the prospective student's social status. In the pre-Reformation period access to education was limited to the political and religious nobility and later to other privileged classes, while the twentieth-century selection procedures have come to be dominated by the student's demonstrated or predicted intellectual status. Where the supply of opportunities has been limited, great emphasis has been placed on the selection of students and the prediction of their performance when exposed to those opportunities. Binet's work in intelligence-test development was directed toward the creation of an instrument that could be used to identify those pupils who were likely to benefit from schooling. His admonitions that education also

Edmund W. Gordon, "Toward a Qualitative Approach to Assessment," in *Briefs*, Report of the Commission on Tests, Vol. II (New York: College Entrance Examination Board, 1970), 42-46. Reproduced by permission.

turn to treatment of those exposed as not likely to succeed were generally ignored. In a period of scarce educational opportunities, Binet's concern for the educability of intelligence did not gain favor. Society found greater utility in the promise of the predictive and selective validity of his new test.

This emphasis on selection and prediction has continued even though the social conditions that gave rise to it have changed. In recent years, we have seen in America a growing concern with universal access to secondary and higher education. The educational requirements of the nation are increasingly defined as post-high school educational opportunities for almost all youth and continued learning for most people. If this trend continues, selection and prediction can no longer be allowed to dominate in the technology of psycho-educational appraisal. Rather, the stage must be shared with an emphasis on *description* and *prescription*—that is, the qualitative description of intellective function leading not to the selection of those most likely to succeed but to the prescription of the learning experiences required to more adequately insure that academic success is possible.

Psychological testing obviously can be used to measure achieved development. From those achievement patterns, subsequent achievement in the same dimensions of behavior under similar learning-experience conditions can be predicted with reasonable validity. Thus people who have learned an average amount during one learning period (high school) may be expected to learn an average amount in the next learning period (college). However, adequate attention has not been given to the facts that psychological testing can be used to describe and qualitatively analyze behavioral function to better understand the processes by which achievement is developed, to describe nonstandard achievements that may be equally functional in subsequent situations requiring adaptation, or to specify those conditions in the interaction between learner and learning experience that may be necessary to change the quality of future achievements.

In the present situation confronting those concerned with access to higher education for larger numbers of young people and for youth from more diverse backgrounds than those from which college students were previously chosen, it is not enough to simply identify the high-risk students. The tasks of assessment and appraisal in this situation are to identify atypical patterns of talent and to describe patterns of function in terms that lead to the planning of appropriate learning experiences. It is therefore recommended that the College Entrance Examination Board immediately:

1. Explore possibilities for adding to its quantitative reports on the performance of students, reports descriptive of the patterns of achievement and function derived from the qualitative analysis of existing tests. The Board's existing instruments should be examined with a view to categorization, factorial analysis, and interpretation to determine whether or not the data of these instruments can be reported in descriptive and qualitative ways, in addition to the traditional quantitative report.

For example, response patterns might be reported differentially for

A. Information recall
   (1) Rote recall
   (2) Associative recall
   (3) Derivative recall

or

B. Vocabulary
   (1) Absolute
   (2) Contextual

2. Explore the development of test items and procedures that lend themselves to descriptive and qualitative analyses of cognitive and affective adaptive functions, in addition to wider specific achievements.

A. In the development of new tests, attention should be given to the appraisal of
   (1) Adaptation in new learning situations
   (2) Problem solving in situations that require varied cognitive skills and styles
   (3) Analysis, search, and synthesis behaviors
   (4) Information management, processing, and utilization skills
   (5) Nonstandard information pools

B. In the development of new procedures, attention should be given to the appraisal of
   (1) Comprehension through experiencing, listening, and looking, as well as reading
   (2) Expression through artistic, oral, nonverbal, and graphic, as well as written symbolization

(3) Characteristics of temperament

(4) Sources and status of motivation

(5) Habits of work and task involvement under varying conditions of demand

C. In the development of tests and procedures designed to get at specific achievements, attention should be given to

   (1) Broadening the varieties of subject matter, competencies, and skills assessed

   (2) Examining these achievements in a variety of contexts

   (3) Open-ended and unstructured probes of achievement to allow for atypical patterns and varieties of achievement

   (4) Assessing nonacademic achievements such as social competence, coping skills, avocational skills, and artistic, athletic, political, or mechanical skills

3. Explore the development of report procedures that convey the qualitative richness of these new tests and procedures to students and institutions in ways that encourage individualized prescriptive educational planning. What is called for is a statement about the nature of adaptive function in each individual that lends itself to planning a way of intervening in and facilitating his development. Patterns of strength and weakness, conditions conducive to successful coping, conditions resulting in congruence and engagement or incongruence and alienation are examples of the kind of information required.

4. Explore the development of research that will add to understanding of the ways in which more traditional patterns of instruction will need to be modified to make appropriate use of wider ranges and varieties of human talent and adaptation in continuing education. It would be relatively useless to identify broader ranges of behavior if these did not have their representation in programs of instruction, and if opportunities for the use of these adaptive patterns in learning were not available to young people. Alongside modification of instruments of assessment and of procedures for appraisal there needs to be a considerable amount of attention given to modifying the curriculum and conditions under which teaching and learning occur.

It must be recognized that the proposals advanced in this brief are, at the present stage of development in human appraisal, very much in the conceptual stage. There is some research but little completed work that can be used to implement such a program. Yet a serious commitment to the achievement of symmetry in the continuing-education entry process, to the broadening of opportunities for access to continuing education, as well as to the greater adaptation of continuing-education programs to the requirements of the extremely varied populations to be served—this commitment demands that answers be provided to the problems implicit in these proposals.

Recommendations

It is recommended that the College Entrance Examination Board:

1. Explore possibilities for adding to its quantitative reports on the performance of students, reports descriptive of the patterns of achievement and function derived from the qualitative analysis of existing tests.

2. Explore the development of test items and procedures that lend themselves to descriptive and qualitative analyses of cognitive and affective adaptive functions, in addition to wider specific achievements.

3. Explore the development of report procedures that convey the qualitative richness of these new tests and procedures to students and institutions in ways that encourage individualized prescriptive educational planning.

4. Explore the development of research that will add to understanding of the ways in which more traditional patterns of instruction will need to be modified to make appropriate use of wider ranges and varieties of human talent and adaptation in continuing education.

Part Three
Tests and the Grouping of Students

7. Using Tests in Grouping Students for Instruction

Ralph W. Tyler

Since the inception of the graded school, teachers have recognized the existence of wide individual differences among the pupils in a given grade, differences that complicated the planning of work and the conducting of instruction. When intelligence and achievement tests first became accepted in American schools, it is understandable that they would be used either along with the teachers' judgments or as the sole criterion for grouping students for instruction.

Dorris Lee states that, by the late 1920's,

the idea of the constancy of the IQ and its implications had taken effect, and schools had widely adopted a horizontal organization which was often called the X, Y, and Z grouping plan. This approach put the highest IQs in the X group, the lowest in the Z, and the "in-betweens" in Y. Pioneered in Cleveland, it was intended that the X group have the content expanded to match their more rapid rate of learning while the content could be cut to bare minimum essentials for the Z group. Educators were so mesmerized by the presumed logic of the scheme that the large majority of schools, countrywide, had adopted this plan or some variant by the early thirties. Then, almost as rapidly as it had developed and much more quietly, the XYZ plan was abandoned almost entirely. Most schools found it simply did not work very well and created personal and social problems to which schools were now beginning to pay attention. Also, with the publication of the Twenty-seventh Yearbook of the National Society for the Study of Education the constancy of the IQ was seriously questioned.[1]

In his essay on "Grouping" Glen Heathers noted, however, that after 1955 there was a "marked resurgence" of interest in ability grouping. In a sample of elementary principals surveyed in 1960, fifty-two percent reported increases in ability grouping in their schools between 1955 and 1961. Even so, according to studies cited by Heathers, it was clear that in 1960 heterogeneous grouping was the commonest form of grouping in elementary schools. Ability grouping tended to occur more frequently in grades seven and eight than in the first six grades of the elementary school.[2]

Two basic assumptions are involved in grouping students for instruction on the basis of test results. The first is that a student learns more efficiently when he is taught in a group relatively homogeneous in terms of ability. The second is that grouping students so as to minimize the variance of their test scores will result in groups that are relatively homogeneous in terms of ability. Both of these assumptions are under attack. A number of research studies present data that demonstrate the difficulty, if not the impossibility, of forming a highly homogeneous group in terms of ability. Other studies show that students who have been taught in ability groups make no more progress in achievement than those heterogeneously grouped. Heathers' summary points up these critical issues. He notes that scores on intelligence tests and on achievement tests are "substantially correlated." But when "pupils are grouped on the basis of IQ alone it has been found that the range of scores on achievement tests is still great." He cites evidence reported by John Goodlad indicating "that dividing students of a grade level into groups on the basis of a measure of general intellectual performance reduces variability in school achievement only about seven percent for a two-group division and seventeen percent for a three-group division."[3]

Not only is it impossible to form highly homogeneous groups in terms of ability but it is doubtful whether any considerable improvement in student learning would result. Heathers goes on to report that "major studies conducted since 1959 have found no clear and consistent effects of ability grouping on students' achievement when total student populations were used." Earlier studies had suggested that both rapid and slow learners profited under ability grouping, but Heathers notes that "recent studies cast serious doubt on this conclusion."[4]

Thus it appears that the usual ways in which tests results are employed to group students for instruction neither produce relatively homogeneous groups nor greatly increase student learning. Furthermore, ability grouping is now under attack by those seeking to eliminate school segregation. They point out that as children from different racial and ethnic groups are enrolled in the same school, they are assigned to segregated classrooms on the basis of test results. In this way the effort to facilitate social interaction among racial and ethnic groups is thwarted by the separation of children into different tracks or so-called ability groups. From his extensive study of equality of educational opportunity, James Coleman concludes that children who have difficulty with school learning make more progress when they are in groups where the majority are relatively successful. His data suggest that the more successful students do not suffer from being in the same classes with those having difficulty.[5] This would seem to support the practice of heterogeneous grouping where each group includes a majority of students who do not have serious difficulties in learning.

The use of ability grouping easily leads to a rigid "tracking system." Heathers cites a 1961 report by John Daniels indicating that a child is likely to remain in the ability "track" to which he was originally assigned. Daniels found that although teachers thought about seventeen percent of students were shifted from one level to another each year, actually the shift was only two percent.[6] This evidence supports the contention of the opponents of "tracking systems" who say that assigning students to a low track on the basis of test results foredooms many children to an inferior education. It also limits their educational choices in high school and thus cuts off opportunities for them to gain admission to college. The effect of such a system should not be assessed solely in terms of its effect on the immediate learning of students but also on the extent to which it narrows educational and life choices of children by serving as a predictor of future educational opportunities and accomplishments.

In spite of the lack of success of many schemes for grouping students for instruction, the efforts to obtain teachable groups will continue where teachers use group instruction and find it difficult to stimulate and guide the learning of children who vary widely in significant characteristics. June Shane and others have identified

forty-two grouping schemes that have been introduced in American
schools or discussed by educational writers between the seventeenth
century and 1970.[7]

Herbert Thelen has done extensive research on the subject of
teachable groups.[8] In a variety of interesting and original experi-
ments he has shown how typical grouping hampers rather than facili-
tates learning. Some of his conclusions are summarized as follows:

> The development of procedures for composing "teachable" or teacher-com-
> patible groups is a fine challenge to diagnostic and trouble-shooting ingenuity. In
> our experiment, we asked each teacher to give us the names of students who got
> a lot out of class and those who got little. We then tested the students of both
> lists on a very comprehensive battery covering everything we could think of that
> might be relevant to personal effectiveness, ranging from projectives to prefer-
> ences for kinds of activities. The responses that differed significantly for the two
> lists were made into a scoring key, different for each teacher, and all the stu-
> dents available in the next year's classes were tested and scored using the com-
> patibility-discriminating key. The teacher's "teachable" class was composed of
> the high scorers.
> This procedure attempts to do the whole job of matching before the classes
> meet. The opposite kind of procedure would be to assign students and teachers
> to each other at random and shift students around from class to class as the need
> arose. A combined technique, beginning with a good guess and then making
> modifications as more information is obtained or as growth occurs to change the
> situation, should be employed, and it should be based on adequate data about
> the effectiveness of each pupil in the social environment of his particular class."[9]

Thelen is describing a way of getting "teachable" groups in the
majority of classrooms where the teacher is the director of student
learning. There are other kinds of classrooms that are more nearly a
microcosm of a democratic society. In such classes, group purposes
are clarified and individual students assigned responsibilities both for
their own learning activities and for helping others.

In summary, the use of test results as a sole basis for grouping
students for instruction seems clearly inappropriate as a means of
composing groups where learning will be improved and teaching will
be easier. American schools appear to be moving away, consciously
or unconsciously, from the practice of segregating students, thus
limiting their opportunities, and toward conscious efforts to increase
student learning and develop a democratic school community. In this
process the devices used to aid in composing groups will need to be
selected or constructed in terms of the information about students

that is required and the way such information is to be used. The use of tests without prior consideration of these matters is no longer justified.

Notes

1. Dorris M. Lee, "Views of the Child," in *The Elementary School in the United States,* Seventy-second Yearbook of the National Society for the Study of Education, Part II (Chicago: the University of Chicago Press, 1973), 167-68.

2. Glen Heathers, "Grouping," in *Encyclopedia of Educational Research,* 4th ed., ed. Robert L. Ebel (London: The Macmillan Co., 1969), 564.

3. *Ibid.*

4. *Ibid.,* 565.

5. James S. Coleman *et al., Equality of Educational Opportunity* (Washington, D.C.: U.S. Government Printing Office, 1966).

6. John C. Daniels, "Effects of Streaming in the Primary School, II: A Comparison of Streamed and Unstreamed Schools," *British Journal of Educational Psychology* 31 (June 1961), 119-27.

7. June Grant Shane *et al., Guiding Human Development: The Counselor and the Teacher in the Elementary School* (Worthington, Ohio: Charles A. Jones Publishing Co., 1971), 383-89.

8. Herbert A. Thelen, *Classroom Grouping for Teachability* (New York: John Wiley and Sons, 1967).

9. Herbert A. Thelen, "The Evaluation of Group Instruction," in *Educational Evaluation: New Roles, New Means,* Sixty-eighth Yearbook of the National Society for the Study of Education, Part II (Chicago: University of Chicago Press, 1969), 136.

Part Four
Criterion-Referenced Testing

As indicated in the Introduction, achievement testing developed as a consequence of the use of tests in World War I to select military personnel for various training and work assignments. The tests were designed to arrange persons in order from those making highest to those making lowest scores. A specified population was employed to furnish norms for the tests. Individual test scores were then interpreted in terms of their relation to the mean and standard deviation of the scores of the norm group. Hence these tests are called "norm-referenced" tests. Today there is increasing demand for the assessment of student achievement of specified educational objectives. Tests designed to furnish information about student achievement of defined educational objectives are called "criterion-referenced" tests.

The debate over the use of norm-referenced versus criterion-referenced tests has even entered the political arena. In explaining his bill in Congress to amend Title I of the Elementary and Secondary Education Act of 1965, the Hon. Albert H. Quie (R-Minnesota), in a speech delivered before the American Association of Colleges for Teacher Education at Chicago in 1973, said,

I have chosen to put my faith in criterion-referenced tests because I believe that through their use we can best escape the onus of comparing the level of achievement of one child and one school against another. If we accept as a federal responsibility the preparation of a child to function in everyday society, to prepare the boys and girls to read a newspaper, interpret road signs and maps, make change in the grocery store, and figure the number of hours worked in a week, then we can avoid the critics who worry about relative content of curriculum teaching styles, etc. I believe that we can arrive at national objectives as valid in Alaska as they are in Florida, for the basic education of our young people. If we confine both the objectives and the measurement of those objectives to language arts and mathematics, we can avoid the problem-plagued areas of social studies, citizenship, psychology, and hard sciences. I recognize them as problem-plagued because they are much more affected by state curricula and local choice.

The following article by Airasian and Madaus gives a helpful explanation of the issues involved in criterion-referenced testing.

8. Criterion-Referenced Testing in the Classroom

Peter W. Airasian and *George F. Madaus*

As education has moved from a luxury to a necessity in American society and as voices for more relevant, less arbitrary stratification systems in education have increased, the problem of grading students has naturally become a focus of attention. For many years student performance has been graded on a norm-referenced, relative basis. A student's grade is assigned on the basis of how he stands in comparison to his peers, not on the basis of any absolute criterion of what his performance is worth. Within the classroom, such grading practices have had two undesirable effects. First, they have given credence to the notion that for success or achievement to mean anything, there must be a reference group of nonattainers. The rewards system engendered by norm-referenced grading *insures* "winners" and "losers" in the achievement race. Second, norm-referenced practices have led to a discrepancy between the rewards system (i.e., grades) and the actual performance of students.

These effects, and a series of concomitant trends to be elaborated later, have led to a renewed interest in a concept of criterion-referenced measurement. In this approach emphasis is placed upon the

Reprinted with permission from *Measurement and Education* 3 (May 1972), 1-7, published by the National Council on Measurement in Education.

question "What has the student achieved?" rather than upon the question "How much has he achieved?"[1] The interpretation of a student's performance in a criterion-referenced situation is absolute and axiomatic, not dependent upon how other learners perform. Either a student is able to exhibit a particular skill, produce a specific product, or manifest a certain behavior, or he is not. Even in situations where some margin of error is permitted, once this margin has been specified, the student's performance can be judged in terms of an "on-off" situation.[2] Both norm- and criterion-referenced systems sort students, but there is an essential difference. In criterion-referenced measurement, interpretation of a student's performance is in no way dependent upon the performance of his classmates. In contrast, the appraisal of norm-referenced performance will differ according to the make-up of the norm group. For example, Mary's scoring higher than 90 percent of a group of academically inferior students on an algebra test will have different implications than her scoring higher than 90 percent in a group of advanced placement students.[3]

Further, and of equal importance, the criterion-referenced approach focuses attention upon a central aspect of the teaching-learning process, namely, the criterion skills. If the criterion behaviors are important, teachers should be concerned with whether the student has achieved them, not with how much he achieved relative to his peers. The teacher should design his instruction in light of the criterion behaviors, and the reward system should reflect this approach.

Background

The distinction between norm- and criterion-referenced tests is not a new one; few ideas in education are. In 1918, E. L. Thorndike observed that:

There are two somewhat distinct groups of educational measurements: one . . . asks primarily how well a pupil performs a certain uniform task; the other . . . asks primarily how hard a task a pupil can perform with substantial perfection, or with some other specified degree of success. The former are allied to the so-called method of average error of the psychologists [norm-referenced]; the latter, to what used to be called the method of "right and wrong cases" [criterion-referenced]. Each of these groups of methods has its advantages, and each deserves extension and refinement though the latter seems to represent the type which will prevail if education follows the course of development of the physical sciences.[4]

Educational measurement, however, did not develop along the lines of the physical sciences, but adopted instead a psychological model based on the concept of individual differences. This psychological lineage, with its emphasis on individual differences, normal distributions, predictions, and the like is a primary reason norm-referenced measurement continues to dominate educational testing to this day.

The work of the Department of Educational Investigation and Measurement of the Boston Public Schools around 1916 offers an excellent example of the course taken by educational measurement in the face of the options Thorndike outlined. Boston teachers were required to draw up a list of words that all students should be able to spell by grade eight. In addition, requirements for English were stated in very precise behavioral terms and all students had to successfully exhibit these behaviors in order to graduate. However, once tests in spelling and English were given to large numbers of students, the percentage passing each item or task began to serve as a "standard by which [the teacher] could judge whether her class [was] above or below the *general standard for the city*" (italics added).[5] It was only a short step from comparing class performance to comparing an individual's performance to such "general city standards." Thus the emphasis shifted from criterion- to norm-referenced evaluation.

The following quote sheds light on some of the reasons underlying such shifts:

Indeed, the measurements which have been made up to this time have more than justified their costs in efforts and money, because they have dispelled forever the idea that schools should produce a uniform product or one that is perfect in its attainment . . . With the theoretical ideal of perfection overthrown, there is now an opportunity to set up rational demands. We can venture to tell parents with assurance that their children in the fifth grade are as good as the average if they misspell fifty percent of a certain list of words. We know this just as well as we know that a certain automobile engine cannot draw a ton of weight up a certain hill. No one has a right to make an unscientific demand of the automobile or of the school.

As soon as school officers recognize the fact *that measurements define for them just how much reasonably may be demanded*, they will be unafraid of measurements (italics added).[6]

Clearly the assumption that most students could be brought to a given level of competence in skill subjects such as spelling was rejected. This rejection was due to a belief widely held at that time that *native* limitations in the ability of children—or poor environmental background—precluded such a goal.[7] A corollary to this view was that reasonable demands upon student learning should be relative rather than absolute. Standardized test makers began to perfect norm-referenced tests to measure individual differences in achievement. Today, virtually all commercially available standardized tests are norm-referenced instruments.

The last three or four years have witnessed a growing interest in criterion-referenced measures, particularly in the classroom context. The interest is predicated upon a series of trends occurring both inside and outside education.

First there has been a growing criticism of testing, the focus of which has been on standardized tests of achievement and ability.[8] This criticism centers upon questions about the relevancy of tasks tested, what education is really about, and the relevancy of sorting people on any bases. However, even one of testing's most vehement critics, John Holt, admits that in at least two circumstances tests are necessary. There is a need in many occupations to demonstrate the ability to meet standards set by the occupation or profession, e.g., symphony orchestra, surgeon, translator, architect, etc. Further, there is a need for tests that allow people to check their progress toward the attainment of a certain skill or knowledge.[9] Both of these functions are better served by criterion-referenced than norm-referenced measures.

A second factor, closely related to the first, is the growing controversy surrounding grades. There is a growing distrust of grades *per se* and a reluctance to want to judge others. Critics argue that the fight for good grades engenders a competitive ethic, emphasizing "winning" the good grade race at the expense of the true purpose of education. The argument proceeds that grades become commodities to be ... [used] in the market place [to bargain] for teacher approval, college admittance, or jobs. The argument concludes, a grade of A or D tells us nothing about what a learner can do, only that he is superior or inferior to some vaguely defined reference group.[10]

A third factor generating interest in criterion-referenced tests has been the growth of the instructional technology movement.[11] Instructional technologists soon realized that norm-referenced tests did not meet their needs in evaluating either individual performance or the efficacy of alternative instructional strategies. A cornerstone in instructional technology is the need for clear statements of instructional objectives. The objectives become a performance standard, for which various instructional strategies are developed. The criterion of success becomes the degree to which the student's performance corresponds to the previously set performance standard.

A fourth factor contributing to the present interest in criterion-referenced measurement is the growing belief on the part of many educators that *all* or *at least most* students can learn, benefit from, or be helped to achieve competency in most subject areas. Educators have argued that the problem of children not learning is not the result of native limitations, but instead a problem of finding better instructional strategies.[12] The assumption that most children can attain a given performance standard, underlies such approaches to instruction as Individually Prescribed Instruction,[13] Performance Contracting,[14] and Mastery Learning.[15] A feature of all such approaches is the use of criterion-referenced measures, both in the formative, ongoing sense, and in the summative, end-of-course sense.[16] Once one accepts the idea that most students can be helped to criterion performance, the emphasis in testing shifts from comparing individuals on a norm-referenced basis to checking and rewarding student learning in terms of that performance. If all attain the criterion, all should receive A's, passes, etc.

These four trends and their wider implications have nurtured the idea of criterion-referenced measurement. It is within the context of these trends and the value position implied by them that the classroom teacher must view criterion-referenced measurement.

Criterion-Referenced Testing and the Classroom Teacher

Is criterion-referenced testing a new concept to the teacher? It could be argued that teachers have always employed implicit, but nonetheless criterion-referenced, standards in their evaluations of pupils. For example, there is little doubt that teachers evaluate such student characteristics as cleanliness, dress, speech patterns, conduct, and verbal fluency against an internal model they have developed as a result of their own socialization process. The model serves as a criterion, a standard, against which each individual student is judged. While the standard is internal, and highly individualistic, it nevertheless plays a powerful part in the formation of teacher expectations about a student's worth, potential, and performance.[17] This type of internal criterion is, of course, different from the common use of the term "criterion-referenced" as found in either the professional literature or in prior sections of this essay. It is not the purpose of this paper to pursue the concept of an internal criterion any further, except to point out that all classrooms are evaluative settings and, while criteria may differ from teacher to teacher, and school to school, in the total evaluative context of the classroom, judgments based on such internal criteria are undoubtedly pervasive and powerful in terms of their effect on teachers and pupils.

Typically, most teachers grade their classroom tests, either explicitly or implicitly, on a scale of zero to one hundred. Each test item is assigned a point value, with the total number of points generally equaling one hundred. Percentages are then translated into A's, B's, C's, D's and F's, often with gradations in between, according to widely accepted convention (90-100 = A; 89-80 = B, etc.). In this system an average grade for a marking period is easily determined.

Is the percentage grading approach an example of criterion-referenced measurement? Lynn's score of 85 percent was, after all, independent of her classmate's performance. She answered 17 of the 20 questions correctly. However, there are several important reasons why this widely accepted marking system does not fit the definition of criterion-referenced measurement described above.

First, the grade or percentage does not describe what Lynn can or cannot do. E. L. Thorndike recognized this problem in 1913 when he observed:

The essential fault of the older schemes for school grades or marks was that the "86" or "B-" did not mean any objectively defined amount of knowledge or power or skill—that, for example, John's attainment of 91 in second-year German did not inform him (or anyone else) about how difficult a passage he could translate; how many words he knew the English equivalents of and how accurately he could pronounce, or about any other fact save that he was supposed to be slightly more competent than someone else marked 89 was, or than he would have been if he had been so marked.[18]

Second, very often teacher-made tests are built without the benefit of a prior statement of the behavioral objectives for the instructional unit. Instead, when some body of content is completed, the test items are constructed and become, after the fact, the *de facto* objectives of the teacher. In order to perform a criterion-referenced measurement one must possess a precise definition of objectives prior to instruction.

Third, even when objectives are clearly defined, the use of a single score to represent performance on a number of different objectives can easily mask what a student can actually do. For example, identical scores of 80 percent often mask the fact that Sarah did poorly on the 8 items measuring Objective A and well on the 8 items measuring Objective B, while the reverse was true for Eileen.

Fourth, the prior problem is compounded when we recognize that the meaning of identical grades on a test purporting to cover the same content can vary widely across teachers because of such factors as different objectives, item selection, and scoring procedures. While it is not necessary—or likely—that every teacher will agree upon the criterion behaviors in English, or math, or reading, it is important that teachers in a department or at a grade level reach some agreement regarding at least minimum skills needed in a subject area. When this task is accomplished, record forms outlining at least the minimal essentials can be developed.

The Mathematics Goal Record Card of the Winnetka, Illinois, Public Schools shown in Figure 8-1 is an example of one type of reporting form that is suited to criterion-referenced measurement. A check indicates that a student has mastered the particular skill. Compare the information provided in this approach to the traditional practice of using a single grade or vague verbal description such as:

distinctly superior work,

above average work,

work of average quality,

meets minimal requirements

unsatisfactory work.

While the goal card could be more specific in terms of defining behaviors (e.g. "understanding") and specifying standards for adequate performance, it does describe what the student can do rather than his rank relative to his peers. The information provided gives a better picture to teachers, students, and parents than vague letter or verbal descriptions. The goal card has a further benefit in that it is more powerful for directing teaching than are the typical norm-referenced categories. Notice also that the goal card can serve to

Recognizes number groups up to 5   ———
Recognizes patterns of objects to 10   ———
Can count objects to 100   ———
Recognizes numbers to 100   ———
Can read and write numerals to 50   ———
Recognizes addition and subtraction symbols   ———
Understands meaning of the equality sign   ———
Understands meaning of the inequality signs   ———
Can count objects:
   by 2's to 20   ———
   by 5's to 100   ———
   by 10's to 100   ———
Recognizes geometric figures:
   triangle   ———
   circle   ———
   quadrilateral   ———
   Recognizes coins (1¢, 5¢, 10¢, 25¢)   ———
Knows addition combinations 10 and under using objects   ———
Knows subtraction combinations 10 and under using objects   ———
Recognizes addition and subtraction vertically and horizontally   ———
Shows understanding of numbers and number combinations
   1. Using concrete objects   ———
   2. Beginning to visualize and abstract   ———
   3. Makes automatic responses without concrete objects ———
Can tell time
   1. Hour   ———
   2. Half hour   ———
   3. Quarter hour   ———
Addition combinations 10 and under (automatic response)   ———
Subtraction combinations 10 and under (automatic response)   ———
Can count to 200   ———
Can understand zero as a number   ———
Can understand place value to tens   ———
Can read and write numerals to 200   ———
Can read and write number words to 20   ———
Use facts in 2-digit column addition (no carrying)   ———
Roman numerals to XII   ———

Figure 8-1. Portion of the mathematics goal record card
of the Winnetka public schools

chart student progress and identify individual needs while instruction is in progress. Most of all, however, it serves to focus attention upon the criterion behaviors.

Two additional distinctions between traditional classroom testing practices and criterion-referenced measurement are related to *when* tests are given and *how* the information derived is used. Teacher-made tests are most often summative measures, in that they are given at the conclusion of a unit of instruction for purposes of grading. Criterion-referenced measurements are amenable to use before instruction begins to properly place students, while instruction is ongoing for purposes of checking progress so that help can be given if necessary (formative testing), and at the end of the unit to see whether students have achieved the criterion.[19] A portrait of group performance on a criterion-referenced test gives information about the efficacy of a particular instructional strategy.

Before describing the steps a teacher or administrator who wishes to employ criterion-based measurement might adopt, a caveat is in order. Criterion-referenced measurement is not a panacea for all the grading or sorting problems in education. The criterion-referenced approach does possess many advantages over norm-referenced approaches within the instructional context. However, criterion-referenced measurement, like all other measurement, is not value free. There is a view of what education is about, what learners are capable of, and the nature of rewards which is implicit in measurement practices based upon absolute rather than normative standards. We have tried to indicate some of these value positions in our discussion of trends which have fostered the criterion-referenced movement. Teachers who opt for criterion-referenced techniques should be aware of the value framework implied. However, advantages of criterion-referenced information in the instructional setting do not rule out the value norm-referenced information can have for administrators, teachers, parents, and students.

Implementing Criterion-Referenced Techniques in the Classroom

It should be recognized at the outset that the steps about to be described reflect the present state of the art and that there are a number of conceptual and methodological issues concerning criterion-referenced testing which remain to be solved.

The first step in implementing criterion-referenced measurement is to develop, prior to instruction, a list of objectives which identify the performances, skills, and products which instruction is designed to help students attain. The list becomes the standard for judging learning success. It is the criterion against which each student's performance will be compared to judge learning adequacy. Implicit in the task of specifying criterion behaviors are two questions: *Who* should do the specifying? and *What* features should the criterion performances manifest?

Probably the teacher, taking into account the level and needs of the students, should have the major say in determining what the criterion behaviors will be. However, very often administrators, parents, and students can provide valuable inputs into this decision-making process. In those cases, where a particular course is a prerequisite to another course or where a number of teachers teach the same course, it is advisable that the criterion behaviors be specified by all teachers concerned. Such a recommendation is not advanced to foster total conformity across classrooms, but only to insure cohesion and direction across teachers teaching the same courses or teachers whose courses are sequential in nature.

The criterion performances, or objectives, should be unambiguously stated. A statement of an objective should contain an operational verb, a verb that describes what the student must do to demonstrate he has learned. Often the conditions under which the behavior is expected to occur should be specified as well. For example,

The student will demonstrate his understanding of the function of the topic sentence in a given paragraph by writing a paragraph about a given subject and underlining the central idea.[20]

When given a newspaper article, the students can distinguish between statements of fact and opinion.

When given a situation he has never encountered, the student can explain what is occurring in terms of Boyle's, Charles', or Bernoulli's Law.

Techniques for writing behavioral objectives are described in many books,[21] and in film strips developed by Vimcet Associates and by General Program Teaching. While the reader should be aware that there are thoughtful critics of the approach to objectives described in the sources listed above,[22] an unambiguous statement of instructional objectives is a necessary first step toward a criterion-based measurement.

The second step in implementing criterion-referenced measurement involves a decision about the standards used to judge whether a student's performance or product indicates mastery of the instructional objectives. Here we need a standard for each objective as well as a standard for the entire set of criterion behaviors. That is, if it is necessary to translate performance on a number of behaviors into pass-fail or yes-no terms, some standard for judging performance across all specific objectives is needed. It is in the area of setting standards, be they for individual objectives or sets of objectives, that criterion-referenced measurement is most in need of research. Thus far, most standards have been arrived at by arbitrary decisions on the part of teachers and researchers. Perfection, that is, perfect mastery, is simply too expensive to obtain. There is evidence[23] that standards set in the area of 80 to 90 percent proficiency are most realistic and meaningful. However, the research is somewhat tentative and for the time being teachers will probably have to rely largely upon their own implicit standards for determining levels of adequacy for criterion behaviors.

Given an objective or set of objectives, there usually will be some standard that will define adequate performance. The standard may involve setting a permissible error rate (i.e., answers correctly 80 percent of the time). Alternatively it may consist of a list of the characteristics associated with an acceptable product or performance. For example, the standard for the previous objective concerning topic sentences and paragraph writing was as follows:

1. The paragraph must be about a single subject.
2. All other sentences in the paragraph must pertain to or support the sentence which the student has underlined.
3. The topic sentence must be underlined.
4. Capitalization and punctuation conventions must be adhered to.

The third step is to devise situations which allow the students a chance to exhibit the desired skill, behavior, or product. In many cases this may mean designing paper and pencil instruments. For example, a paper and pencil test is required to assess the following objective: given a set of 10 problems calling for dividing mixed fractions, the student is able to correctly solve the problems with 90 percent accuracy. In form, the items look identical to items developed for a norm-referenced arithmetic test. Further, the item writing techniques do not differ for norm- versus criterion-referenced tests. The reader is referred to Thorndike[24] for a detailed description of item-writing techniques. The essential difference lies in whether the items are used to determine whether a student has mastered division of mixed numbers or where he stands relative to his peers on this skill.

It should be pointed out here that the use of a criterion-referenced approach does not automatically make the testing situation diagnostic, except insofar as it identifies a particular skill a student possesses or fails to possess. In our example of dividing mixed numbers, suppose two students each answered correctly 7 of the 10 items. The conclusion is that the students have not reached the prespecified criterion and therefore have not mastered the arithmetic skill in question. By itself this piece of information is of little diagnostic value. Martha might have missed three items because she incorrectly changed the mixed numbers to fractions while Anthony missed three items because of mistakes in simple multiplication. The point is criterion-referenced information is not intrinsically diagnostic if one stops with an "on-off" statement of results. Popham and Husek[25] describe the ideal criterion-referenced test as one in which a person's score exactly describes his whole response pattern. No such test is in sight. The point is, then, that generally the more complex the objective, the less prescriptive the test results are likely to be.

There have been efforts in the past few years to specify not only criterion behaviors in school subjects, but also ordering or sequential relationships between behaviors.[26] A body of content or a task is analyzed to determine a sequence in which performances are identified as prerequisites to or necessary products of other performances. Tests based upon such sequences are criterion-referenced, but they also possess a diagnostic value in that they are often able to shed light on the question of why a student failed to demonstrate competence on a given objective, i.e., he failed a prerequisite criterion behavior.

In building a paper and pencil criterion-referenced instrument, all of the items should represent the behavior or behaviors defined in the criterion performances so that accurate inference can be made from test results. Tyler,[27] however, points out that there is little theory "to aid in the construction of relatively homogeneous samples of exercises faithfully reflecting an educational objective." Until such techniques are developed, teachers will have to judge the validity of the items or exercises relative to the objective in question. The bases for this judgment can be expert opinion, experience, the face validity of the items, or group consensus. It is precisely on these bases that teachers judge item adequacy at present.

For many objectives, paper and pencil tests will be inappropriate. Actual situations in which the students' performance is observed and rated are required. For example, to determine whether a child has sufficient eye-hand coordination to handle scissors is best measured by giving the child a piece of paper and a pair of scissors. Thus, to assess this capability, Kamii describes the following measurement technique and criteria:

Give a piece of paper and a pair of scissors to a child and ask him to cut the paper (a) in any way he likes and (b) on a line you have drawn on the paper.

Criteria:
    Cutting in any way the child likes:
    — Cuts easily without any trouble
    — Cuts with some slight difficulty
    — Cuts with considerable difficulty
    — Simply cannot cut and appears to be "all thumbs"
    Cutting in a line: (The following criteria refer not to the child's general ability to use scissors but to his specific ability to cut along a given line.)
    — Cuts easily and accurately on the line
    — Cuts easily but with a deviation within ¼ inch from the line
    — Cuts with some difficulty with a deviation of more than ¼ inch from the line.[28]

A moment's reflection will reveal that it is impossible to convert this measurement, either implicitly or explicitly, into a norm-referenced scale. Even though two students attain criterion performance, it is often difficult to avoid making comparisons between students on the basis of the speed, fluency, smoothness, or adroitness with which they attained the criterion. Dewey[29] points out that valuing has two aspects, one of prizing, the other appraising. The latter involves comparison and is concerned with the relational property of objects. Whether this relational aspect can be limited to the criterion in question or whether it also inadvertently spills over into comparisons between people is something one must be aware of.

In still other circumstances student products might have to be critically examined in order to infer whether or not the student has in fact attained the required skill or competency. Baldwin[30] describes such rating scale for a woodworking project in vocational education. In terms of rating scales Baldwin points out that the teacher using a rating scale should also demonstrate the objectivity of the instrument for the situation for which it was designed by determining both inter and intra rater consistency in light of the criterion performance.

In summary, any classroom approach to criterion-referenced measurement should include the following steps:

1. competencies to be demonstrated by the student must be stated in explicit terms
2. criteria identifying levels or characteristics of successful accomplishment of the competencies must be made explicit
3. situations in which the student can demonstrate his competency or lack of competency must be developed
4. judgments of any student's learning success must be made in light of the predefined competencies, not in relation to other students' performances.

Conclusion

Criterion-referenced testing is not a panacea for all the grading and sorting problems which exist in education. More thoughtful reflection and research is required before all the difficulties associated with criterion-based measurement are resolved. However, the criterion-referenced approach serves two very valuable functions within the instructional context. First, it directs attention to the performances and behaviors which are the main purpose of instruction. Secondly, it rewards students on the basis of their attainment relative to these criterion performances rather than relative to their peers. Under such conditions rewards are distributed on the basis of achievement *vis à vis* the aims of instruction and the frequently meaningless distinctions made between students on the basis of "how much" are replaced by a reward system based upon what has actually been attained.

Notes

1. J. H. Block (ed.), *Mastery Learning: Theory and Practice* (New York: Holt, Rinehart and Winston, 1971).

2. W. J. Popham and T. R. Husek, "Implications of Criterion-referenced Measurement," in W. J. Popham (ed.), *Criterion-referenced Measurement* (Englewood Cliffs, N.J.: Educational Technology Publishers, 1971), 17-37.

3. Benjamin S. Bloom, J. Thomas Hastings, and G. F. Madaus, *Handbook on Formative and Summative Evaluation of Student Learning* (New York: McGraw-Hill, 1971).

4. E. L. Thorndike, "The Nature, Purposes and General Methods of Measurements of Educational Products," in *The Measurement of Educational Products*, Seventeenth Yearbook of the National Society for the Study of Education, Part II (Bloomington, Ill.: Public School Publishing Company, 1918), 16-24.

5. F. W. Ballow, "Work of the Department of Educational Investigation and Measurement, Boston, Massachusetts," in *Standards and Tests for the Measurement of the Efficiency of Schools and School Systems*, Fifteenth Yearbook of the National Society for the Study of Education, Part I (Bloomington, Ill.: Public School Publishing Company, 1916), 61-68.

6. C. H. Judd, "A Look Forward," in *The Measurement of Educational Products*, 152-60.

7. *Ibid.*

8. B. Hoffman, *The Tyranny of Testing* (New York: Collier Books, 1962); J. W. Holt, *On Testing* (Cambridge, Mass.: Pinck Leodas Associates, 1968); Ivan Illich, *Deschooling Society* (New York: Harper and Row, 1971); Charles E. Silberman, *Crisis in the Classroom* (New York: Vantage Books, 1970).

9. J. W. Holt, *op. cit.*, 1.

10. J. Farber, *The Student as Nigger* (New York: Pocket Books, 1969); New University Conference, *De-grading Education* (Bloomington, Ind.: Jeff Sharlett Chapter of the New University Conference, 1972).

11. R. M. Gagne, *The Conditions of Learning* (New York: Holt, Rinehart and Winston, 1965); R. Glaser, "A Criterion-referenced Test," in W. J. Popham (ed.), *Criterion-referenced Measurement*, 41-51; F. Mechner, "Science Education and Behavioral Technology," in R. Glaser (ed.), *Teaching Machines and Programmed Learning, II* (Washington, D.C.: National Education Association, 1965) 441-507.

12. Benjamin S. Bloom, "Learning for Mastery," *UCLA-CSEIP Evaluation Comment*, 1 (No. 2, 1968); J. S. Bruner, *The Process of Education* (Cambridge, Mass.: Harvard University Press, 1960); John B. Carroll, "A Model of School Learning," *Teachers College Record* 64 (May 1963), 723-33; J. H. Block, "Criterion-referenced Measurement: Potential," *School Review* 79 (February 1971) 289-97; S. T. Mayo, "Mastery Learning and Mastery Testing," *Measurement in Education* 1 (March 1970), 1-4.

13. C. M. Lindvall and R. Cox, *Evaluation as a Tool in Curriculum Development: The IPI Evaluation Program*, (Chicago: Rand McNally, 1970).

14. Leon Lessinger, *Every Kid a Winner* (New York: Simon and Schuster, 1970).

15. J. H. Block (ed.), *Mastery Learning*.

16. P. W. Airasian, "The Role of Evaluation in Mastery Learning," in J. H. Block (ed.) *Mastery Learning*, 81-93; Bloom, Hastings, and Madaus, *op. cit.*

17. P. W. Airasian, T. Kallaghan, and G. F. Madaus, "Standardized Test

Information, Teacher Expectancies and the Rhetoric of Evaluation," working paper for a Conference on the Design of a Societal Experiment on the Consequences of Testing, Dublin, Ireland, 1971.

18. Glaser, "A Criterion-referenced Test," 48-49.

19. P. W. Airasian and G. F. Madaus, "Functional Types of Student Evaluation," *Measurement and Evaluation in Guidance* 4 (January 1972), 221-33.

20. Center for the Study of Evaluation, "Language Arts, 4-6," *Instructional Objectives Exchange* (1970), 127.

21. N. E. Gronlund, *Stating Behavioral Objectives for Classroom Instruction* (New York: The Macmillan Co., 1970); R. F. Mager, *Preparing Instructional Objectives* (Palo Alto, Calif.: Fearon Publishers, 1962); Bloom, Hastings, and Madaus, *op. cit.*

22. Elliot W. Eisner, "Instructional and Expressive Objectives; Their Formation and Use in Curriculum," in *Instructional Objectives*, American Educational Research Association Monograph on Curriculum Evaluation (Chicago: Rand McNally, 1969), 1-31; W. E. Doll, "A Methodology of Experience: An Alternative to Behavioral Objectives," paper read at the 1971 Annual Meeting of the American Educational Research Association, New York, 1971; H. S. Broudy, "Can Research Escape the Dogma of Behavioral Objectives?" *School Review* 79 (November 1970), 43-56.

23. J. H. Block, "Student Evaluation: Towards the Setting of Mastery Performance Standards," paper read at the 1972 Annual Meeting of the American Educational Research Association, Chicago, 1972.

24. Robert L. Thorndike (ed.), *Educational Measurement* (Washington, D. C.: American Council on Education, 1971).

25. W. J. Popham and T. R. Husek, *op. cit.*

26. P. W. Airasian, "A Study of the Behaviorally Dependent, Classroom Taught Task Hierarchies," Educational Technology Research Report Series, Number 3, 1971; R. M. Gagne, *op. cit.*; L. B. Resnick, "Design of an Early Learning Curriculum," University of Pittsburgh Learning Research and Development Center, Working Paper 16, 1967.

27. R. W. Tyler, "Changing Concepts of Educational Evaluation," in R. Stake (ed.), *Perspectives of Curriculum Evaluation*, American Educational Research Association Monograph Series on Curriculum Evaluation (Chicago: Rand McNally, 1967), 14.

28. C. K. Kamii, "Evaluation of Learning in Preschool Education," in Bloom, Hastings, and Madaus, *op. cit.*, 308.

29. J. Dewey, *Theory of Valuation* (Chicago: University of Chicago Press, 1939).

30. T. S. Baldwin, "Evaluation of Learning in Industrial Education," in Bloom, Hastings, and Madaus, *op. cit.*, 855-905.

Part Five
Assessing the Educational Achievement
of Institutions

The term "educational accountability" is frequently heard today. It is accompanied by a growing demand for dependable information about what students are learning in schools. Some of the obvious reasons for this emphasis are:

1. Rapidly rising school costs have stimulated urgent public concern to determine what kind of return is being obtained from these educational expenditures
2. The development and installation of new and often expensive instructional programs has invited questions about whether students are better off or not as a result of them
3. Educational administrators require information in order to make decisions regarding the allocation of resources.

At no time in recent history have educational institutions been so pressed to account for what they are doing.

Assessment activities are currently being carried out at a number of levels. At the national level the National Assessment of Educational Progress (NAEP) has been conducting an ongoing program to assess what students have learned in various curricular areas at different age levels. The following papers by Ralph W. Tyler, Carmen J. Finley, and George H. Johnson present information on the background and purposes of this enterprise, the nature of the measures and how they are being employed, and the uses being made of the results.

At the state level, a variety of approaches to assessment are being considered and tried. Dyer and Rosenthal present the results of a survey of state assessment efforts along with a discussion of some emerging problems. Information about current assessment efforts in several states is also presented.

At the local level, assessment efforts are varied. The final section of this chapter contains a discussion of some of the considerations involved in the assessment of education at the district and building levels.

9. Assessing Education at the National Level

Why Evaluate Education?

Ralph W. Tyler

The need for a continuing assessment of the progress of education in this country arises from the great demands which are now being made upon education. Most of the goals we seek as a people require education as a means of reaching them. To meet these demands, the American people are furnishing far greater resources for our educational institutions than have ever been available before. Yet much more is being requested. It is clear that the resources required cannot be provided except by using the greatest care in their allocation and use. The public needs to understand more adequately what educational progress is being made and where the critical problems lie on which much greater attention and effort must be focused. The public needs this kind of information in order to give intelligent backing for the decisions that must be made to use resources wisely to produce maximum results.

We have data of this kind about other matters of public concern, such as our population growth, its rate of increase, the extent and direction of migration; about the income levels of our people and the incidence of disease. Need for this information was recognized a

Reprinted with permission from *Compact* 6 (February 1972), 3-4.

generation ago and, over the years, means for obtaining the information were worked out and are continually being refined. We now have useful, comprehensive, and comparable data regarding types of morbidity and mortality for various ages, occupations, regions, and the like. We know the diseases that are currently the chief causes of death in different age groups, and in different occupations and income categories. We have helpful estimates of production, prices, and unemployment ratios. These kinds of data enable the public to understand progress and problems in these fields, and they furnish perspectives from which to make decisions.

But before the advent of the National Assessment, we had no comprehensive and dependable data about the educational attainments of our people. The data available at the state and national level have been reports on numbers of schools, buildings, teachers, and pupils, and about the monies expended, but we have not had sound and trustworthy information on educational results. Because dependable data were not available, personal views, distorted reports, and journalistic impressions have been the sources of public opinion, and the schools have been attacked by some and defended by others without having necessary evidence to support either claim.

Teaching Johnny to Read

For example, some years ago a book entitled "Why Johnny Can't Read" had a great influence on public opinion, without any evidence being presented as to how many Johnnies can't read, and in what population groups is there a considerable fraction of nonreaders. It turned out that the effect of this arousal of public opinion was to redesign programs for teaching reading largely in schools in which most children were learning to read, rather than focusing the added effort and expenditure on schools where there were serious problems in learning to read. Had data been available at that time on the reading achievements of American children, the public would have had information about the incidence of inadequate reading abilities and could have supported efforts to attack the problems where they were rather than to have stimulated programs that did not reach the schools where they were needed.

Some persons question the statement that the public has not had comprehensive and dependable information about what American children and youth have learned. They know that educational achievement tests have been on the market for 50 years and that they are used widely. Would not the compilation of the scores on standard achievement tests furnish the data the public needs?

The standard achievement tests in common use do not give a dependable measure of what children have learned. They are not constructed to do so. A typical achievement test is explicitly designed to furnish scores that will arrange the pupils on a line from those most proficient in the subject to those least proficient. The final test questions are selected from a much larger initial number on the basis of tryouts and are the ones which most sharply distinguished pupils in the tryouts who made high scores on the total test from those who made low scores. Test questions are eliminated if most pupils can answer them or if few pupils can answer them, since these do not give much discrimination.

As a result, a large part of the questions retained for the final form of a standard test are those that 40 to 60 percent of the children are able to answer. There are very few questions that represent the things being learned either by the slower learners or the more advanced ones. If a less advanced student is actually making progress in his learning, the typical standard test furnishes so few questions that represent what he has been learning that it will not afford a dependable measure for him. The same holds true for advanced learners.

The Score's Not the Answer

This is not a weakness of the test in serving the purpose for which it was designed. The children who made lower scores had generally learned fewer things in this subject than those who made higher scores and could, therefore, be dependably identified as less proficient. Furthermore, a good standard test has been administered to one or more carefully selected samples, usually national, regional, or urban samples, of children in the grade for which the test was designed. The scores obtained from these samples provide norms for the test against which a child's score can be related. These tests thus provide dependable information about where the child stands in his total test performance in relation to the norm group. But when one seeks to find out whether a student who made a low score has learned certain things during the year, the test does not include enough questions covering the material on which he was working to furnish a dependable answer to that question.

The National Assessment has been designed to sample the things which children and youth are expected to learn in school, and to find out what proportion of our people are learning these things. The instruments used in the assessment are not tests which give each person a score or a grade. They are exercises that children, youth, and young adults are given. Instead of a score, the results are reported in terms of the percent of each population group that was able to perform the exercise. These exercises show the public both what our children are learning and how many are learning each thing. The public is thus able to make judgments about each exercise. How important is this for children to learn? And, in what regions and other circumstances are most children learning this, and in what circumstances are only part of the children learning?

Schools Must Teach Students, Not Merely "Sort" Them

The purpose of the National Assessment is closely related to the current call for accountability in education. In contrast to earlier years when schools were expected to give major emphasis to sorting pupils so that only a fraction of those who entered school at six years of age would graduate from high school, the discussion of accountability today emphasizes the purpose of the school as learning rather than sorting. It seeks to hold the school accountable for educating all the children, not simply furnishing opportunities for the elite. In meeting the demand that all children learn what the school is expected to teach, data are needed about what is being learned by all parts of the population. Schools are discovering that the commonly used standard tests do not show what pupils have learned nor what proportion of the children has learned each of the things the school is teaching. An increasing number of schools is asking for exercises like those developed in the National Assessment so that they can use them as part of their programs for accountability.

Such instruments could furnish information about the progress and problems of the school in providing the kind and quality of service that the public is now expecting. A constructive dialogue can then be maintained with the community regarding the educational objectives, the efforts the school is making to reach these objectives, the progress pupils are making in their learning, the difficulties being encountered, and the steps being taken to overcome these difficulties. Ample information on these matters can make the dialogue a constructive one and can reassure the general public about the integrity of the school in meeting its responsibilities.

In this program for accountability carried on in the local school district, the National Assessment not only furnishes an example of the kinds of instruments to be used to appraise the results of the school's efforts, but the reports of the National Assessment also give a helpful background for the dialogues with the public. The clientele of the local school sometimes places the blame for difficulties in pupil learning upon the teachers and principals without knowing that certain problems are characteristic of the entire nation or region. Because the National Assessment provides background data, the public can gain a broader perspective from which to view the local problems. There will be less tendency to attack the local schools groundlessly because the public will see that most difficult educational problems are not localized and cannot be blamed upon a particular administrator or set of teachers.

In summary, the National Assessment provides a means of helping the public understand the results being achieved by our educational system and the problems encountered. It furnishes a basis for intelligent examination of the situation and helps to identify the places on which to focus more effective efforts.

Not Just Another Standardized Test

Carmen J. Finley

Every year, billions of dollars are spent on education in the United States on buildings, on teachers' salaries, on curriculum planning— but very little is known about the effectiveness of this expenditure. The purpose of the National Assessment of Educational Progress is to

Reprinted with permission from *Compact* 6 (February 1972), 9-12.

gather information which will help answer the question, "How much good is the expenditure doing, in terms of what young Americans know and can do?"

National Assessment, as a nationwide project collecting information about certain groups of young Americans, will, over a period of time, provide valuable information needed to make wise decisions about the allocation of our resources within the field of education.

Concern over the need for this type of national information first began during the time Francis Keppel was U. S. commissioner of education (1962-65). Keppel discovered that, in the original charter of the U. S. Office of Education (1867), a charge was given to the U. S. commissioner to determine the progress of education. This provided the initial impetus for National Assessment.

After a number of conferences and discussions initiated by Commissioner Keppel, John W. Gardner, then president of Carnegie Corporation, asked a distinguished group of Americans to form the Committee on Assessing the Progress of Education under the chairmanship of Ralph W. Tyler (then director of the Center for Advanced Study in the Behavioral Sciences, Stanford, California). Their charge was to consider development of an assessment program which would provide benchmarks of educational progress as a basis for evaluating the changing educational needs of our society over the years. Specifically, they were to:

1. Determine how a national assessment of educational progress could be designed;
2. Develop and test instruments and procedures for the assessment; and
3. Develop a plan for conducting the assessment.

Four years of work, financed by the Carnegie Corporation of New York and the Fund for the Advancement of Education of the Ford Foundation, went into defining goals and developing measuring instruments to answer these questions. The work was done in consultation with subject-matter experts, leading educators, and interested laymen. Ten subject-matter areas were defined for assessment: art, career and occupational development, citizenship, literature, mathematics, music, reading, science, social studies, and writing.

In 1969-70 the first actual assessment was made—in the areas of citizenship, science, and writing. Last year, reading and literature were assessed. Social studies and music are now underway, and preparations are being made for the assessment of mathematics and science next year. By 1974-75, all 10 areas will have been assessed once, and several areas will have been assessed twice.

The exercises in each area are designed to measure what groups of people know and can do. Data in each subject area are collected for:

Four age levels [9, 13, 17, and young adult (26-35)]

Seven types of community (inner city,* big city,** urban fringe, affluent suburb, medium-sized cities, small town and rural, farm rural)

Four geographical regions (Northeast, Southeast, Central, West)

Four educational levels of parents (not more than 8th grade, more than 8th grade but less than high school graduation, high school graduation, some formal education beyond high school)

Color (Black, White, Other)

Sex

For the first time in American education, there is a plan to systematically sample what people know and can do and to report the results to all people involved directly or indirectly in the ongoing process of improving education.

Basic Differences between National Assessment and Standardized Testing Programs

There are seven basic distinctions between the National Assessment program and traditional standardized testing programs used by most schools. These differences are summarized in Table 9-1 . . .

Table 9-1. Characteristics of the national assessment program as compared with traditional standardized testing programs

National Assessment Program	*Standardized Testing Program*
1. National Assessment exercises measure how well students as a group achieve desirable goals.	Standardized tests compare students with the average performance of other students.
2. The time allotted to a given learning area ranges from six to eight hours each.	The time allotted to a given subject ranges from about 30 minutes to 70 minutes each.

*Inner city is the 10 percent extreme impoverished area of *big* cities.

**Big city is all other areas excluding the 10 percent extreme.

3. National Assessment administers exercises to groups no larger than 12 and to individuals by interview.	Standardized tests are generally administered to total classes or groups of classes in a central location.
4. Exercises use a wide variety of stimuli and approaches often requiring the student to perform or to provide the correct response rather than just recognize it.	Test items are generally confined to that paper-and-pencil variety which can be scored by machine.
5. Exercises are prepared for the "high," the "average," and the "low" ability students.	Items are aimed at the "average" child.
6. Total scores, which reflect the number of students who got the correct answer, are given to each exercise. People do not receive total scores.	Total scores reflect the number of correct answers a student gives.
7. Results are reported on an exercise-by-exercise basis.	Results are reported in relation to a standardization group.

Defining Goals versus Comparison with an Average

In the National Assessment program specific objectives or goals are defined and exercises are written which determine how well these goals are being met. For example, in citizenship a major objective is to "Support Rights and Freedoms of All Individuals." One specific way in which a person might meet this goal is to defend the right of a person with very unpopular views to express his opinion and support the right of "extreme" (political or religious) groups to express their views in public.

One exercise which was written to try to tell whether or not this objective was being met is as follows:

Below are three statements which make some people angry. Mark each statement as to whether you think a person on radio or TV should or should not be allowed to make these statements:
    "Russia is better than the United States."
    "Some races of people are better than others."
    "It is not necessary to believe in God."

This is the goal-oriented approach. The objectives or goals represent a kind of standard which is considered desirable to achieve. The exercises, if they are good measures, tell to what extent the goals are being achieved. This approach tells very specifically what a person knows or can do.

In the norm-referenced approach which is typical of standardized testing programs used by most schools, there are no standards, although the results are sometimes misinterpreted in such a way as to imply there are standards.

The main purpose of the traditional standardized testing program is to place individuals taking the test in rank order from high to low. The results can then be used to counsel or to group youngsters for instructional purposes or to select them for special programs or for college entrance, etc. Standardized tests are also used to evaluate instructional programs or schools or districts or even whole states but the results will only tell whether or not the program (school or district or state) is above or below the average of the group upon which the test was standardized. It will not tell what people know or can do, except in a very limited sense.

Amount of Coverage

The assessment of any subject area for National Assessment is as comprehensive as possible. Every effort is made to measure each of the objectives in each area. The minimal amount of material needed to do this generally ranges from about six to eight hours of actual assessment time. This does not mean that any one person is subjected to so many questions. The total amount of materials is divided into 35-minute units (for in-school administration) and 45-minute units (for administration outside of school). No youngster in school takes more than one unit, and adults may elect to take up to four units. Since National Assessment is interested only in group results, it is possible to portion out the materials in this manner and keep the demands placed upon any youngster or school within reasonable limits.

In contrast, the typical standardized test allots approximately 30 to 70 minutes worth of testing time per subject area, and each person takes the same test as every other person. Frequently a number of subject areas are gathered together into a battery, and the total battery may be administered over a period of two or three days.

Type of Administration

National Assessment uses many traditional paper-and-pencil exercises (items), but they are administered in groups of not more than

12 youngsters so that maximum control can be gained over the assessment situation. In addition, all exercises administered in groups use a paced tape, both to instruct the youngsters and to read the actual questions (except in the area of reading). Previous research has shown that the usual disadvantage which poor readers or bilingual children have in testing situations can be somewhat alleviated through these methods.

In addition many National Assessment exercises are administered to one child at a time by an interviewer. These are generally exercises of a more complicated nature which attempt to measure the youngsters' thought processes (reasoning and thinking logically, drawing inferences, reaching conclusions, analyzing and synthesizing different points of view) or their ability to perform in some way (i.e., play a musical instrument, demonstrate a scientific principle using apparatus, use a typewriter, etc.).

Traditional testing programs, on the other hand, are typically administered in larger groups, and each youngster must rely on his own reading ability to understand the meaning of the question. Individual testing of students is generally reserved for the small percentage of youngsters who exhibit some type of psychological problems.

Variety of Materials Used and Associated Scoring Problems

Because many of National Assessment's exercises are more complicated than the usual standardized test, the scoring is often more complicated. Standardized tests are generally objectively scored; that is, they can be scored by machine at a very rapid rate. Machine scoring is feasible only if the youngster has a limited number of answers presented to him from which he selects. While National Assessment does use some exercises of this type, many are open-ended, or require the youngster to produce and write out his answer rather than just recognize it from among other wrong choices. In addition, exercises which require him to perform in some manner must be judged in a different way. For these more complicated materials very detailed scoring criteria and keys are developed on the basis of field testing which precedes the assessment. Then specially qualified and trained persons are required to do the scoring.

Difficulty of Materials

National Assessment by design set out to assess what the most capable person could do, what the average person could do, and what the least able person could do at each age level in the assessment. Materials, therefore, had to be developed which aimed specifically at each of these levels. Results of the first year of assessment indicated that the materials did cover the full range of ability at each age.

In contrast, the typical standardized test best measures within the average range. This is a technical necessity for the purpose it serves— to discriminate among youngsters and place them in rank order. Not infrequently the best students will "go off the top of the test" or the poorest will "fall off the bottom"—thus neither one is adequately measured.

What Scores Are Important

In National Asssessment scores are not obtained on individuals. Since any one individual takes only a small fraction of the total amount of materials, scores for individuals would really have no meaning. The scores that are important are those which tell what a group of people did on any given exercise. This gives a kind of item-analysis on a national level and, in keeping with the goals of the program, tells what people know or can do across the nation.

In the traditional testing program items are added and a total score (or set of subtest scores) is obtained for each person. This score is then compared with scores obtained on a standardization group, and it is possible to tell whether the individual ranks high, average, or low with respect to that group.

How Results Are Reported

As indicated above, the results for National Assessment are reported by exercise, i.e., how groups of people perform on each exercise.

The free speech exercise which was given earlier in this article was reported as follows:

Believe a person on radio or TV should
be allowed to say:

	Age		
	13	*17*	*Adult*
"Russia is better than the United States."	21%	49%	56%
"Some races of people are better than others."	16%	31%	37%
"It is not necessary to believe in God."	25%	49%	55%
Would allow all three statements	6%	22%	32%

In the traditional testing program reports generally show only the relationship of the student or group to the standardization group. The student or group will be above or below "norm." Since the norm represents an average performance, in effect, the report will show how far above or below average the student or group happens to be on that particular test.

In summary, there are a number of fairly major distinctions which set National Assessment apart from traditional standardized testing programs. This is not to say that one is better than the other, but they do serve distinctly different purposes.

Making the Data Work

George H. Johnson

"Is anyone using it?" is an increasingly frequent question from National Assessment audiences. Since the eventual success of National Assessment must be measured in terms of its impact on educational practice, content, and decision making, this, of course, is very appropriate.

Before answering this question, however, it is necessary to identify what there is about National Assessment that is capable of being

Reprinted with permission from *Compact* 6 (February 1972), 29-30.

"used." National Assessment "products" are of two basic types. The first of these consists of the objectives, procedures, criterion-referenced exercises, sampling plans, etc., which together provide a model, technology, and materials for conducting assessments at state and local levels. The second applicable output is made up of data on achievement in each assessed subject area, which can be analyzed and reported in various ways. The potential for "use" or application, and the audiences (or users) involved, may be quite different for these two kinds of National Assessment "products."

On December 2, 1971, the Education Commission of the States [ECS] Steering Committee approved the recommendation of the NAEP Policy Committee that an Office of Utilization be created in response to the need to effectively use and apply the results of NAEP. Planning is currently under way for establishing several projects aimed at furthering the utilization function.

Furthest along in development is the use of the model, technology, and materials developed by National Assessment. Available are: (1) statements of objectives for each of the ten subjects under assessment, with procedures for achieving agreement among specialists, educators, and representatives of the lay public; (2) methods and guidelines for developing criterion-referenced exercises to measure the objectives; (3) a sampling design and administrative procedures for implementing the design; (4) a selection of the actual criterion-referenced exercises used in earlier assessments. In this area, NAEP is trying to identify present applications, such as, use of the objectives in local goal setting, adoption of the NAEP model for state or local assessments and administration of the released exercises at a state or local level to generate comparative data. Several such applications are known to be in progress, and NAEP is rendering assistance in several of these areas. However, the extent and range of such current applications need to be determined to aid in planning future utilizations.

In addition, materials are being prepared to inform potential users about NAEP and to provide the knowledge and materials needed for assessment applications. Materials include modifications to the National Assessment model which is adaptable to state and local circumstances, development of cost models and unit costs for the National Assessment approach, and making released exercises in subject areas available to potential users.

Still further, active dissemination efforts—publications, presentations at meetings, consultations with state and local educators—will be stepped up in order to make utilizations more feasible. Special projects, such as workshops for state and local assessment specialists, establishment of experimental and pilot or demonstration schools or school districts to apply the National Assessment model and materials, are in the planning stage.

Use for Educational Improvement

In contrast to the above, utilizations of the data reported through National Assessment are envisioned as taking a different form. These kinds of utilizations require data interpretation and their implications for education. In contrast to utilization which generates information, this utilization takes already generated information and uses it for educational improvement and decision making. With the projected completion of baseline reporting in science, citizenship, and writing, the entire sets of National Assessment data on achievement in three subject areas will be available for the first time. Data in other subject areas will be available as each successive year of the project is completed.

NAEP staff has traditionally considered this area as being outside the scope of its mission. However, NAEP staff can serve as a catalytic influence to promote interpretive activities, and it is this kind of an active role which it will assume. In line with its mission, a number of activities are contemplated, such as sponsoring work groups, reaction panels, or study groups made up of educational specialists and lay people to study and interpret results and suggest implications; working with curriculum projects and publishers of instructional materials to make modifications and reemphases suggested by the data; encouraging professional education organizations to assume an active role in interpreting and implementing National Assessment results and other activities of a comparable nature.

Also in line with this aspect of the applications program will be the redesigning of NAEP reports to facilitate their use and interpretation as well as active dissemination through publication, conferences, etc. of known and potential applications.

National Assessment Utilizations, still in its formative stages, has generated considerable excitement about the possibilities of improving American education. The participation of educational decision-makers, curriculum specialists, instructional designers, and concerned laymen in this important effort is actively solicited.

10. Assessing Education at the State Level

Overview of the Survey Findings

Henry S. Dyer and *Elsa Rosenthal*

I. Introduction

In the middle 1960's three events in the national scene had a considerable impact in changing ways of thinking about educational assessment at the state level. The first was the formation in 1964 of the Exploratory Committee on the Assessment of Progress in Education, which eventuated in the National Assessment program now underway.[1] The second event was the enactment of the Elementary and Secondary Education Act of 1965, which included a requirement that school systems assess by objective means the effects on student achievement produced by federally funded programs for the educationally deprived.[2] The third was the publication in 1966 of the Coleman report on *Equality of Educational Opportunity*,[3] which attempted to assess, again in terms of measured pupil achievement, the quality of service the schools were supplying to various segments of the population.

A common element is discernible in all three of these efforts: namely, an insistence that, in assessing the performance of the

Henry S. Dyer and Elsa Rosenthal, "Overview of the Survey Findings," in *State Educational Assessment Programs* (Princeton, N.J.: Educational Testing Service, 1971), ix-xix. Copyright © 1971 by Educational Testing Service. All rights reserved. Reprinted by permission.

schools, major attention must be given to measuring the performance of the children who attend the schools. This approach points up a sharp contrast to the traditional methods of school assessment that had usually appraised the quality of educational programs and services primarily in terms of the quality of school plant and facilities, the paper credentials of professional personnel, the number of dollars expended per pupil, and the like.

Although the three national undertakings mentioned above generated a considerable amount of public controversy, the essential merit of the approach they took has become increasingly clear to educational policy makers at the state level. As a consequence, there has been a growing interest among state authorities in trying to use similar methods for determining what state and local services tend to be most effective in helping students learn.

The states have not been strangers to the concept of measurement in education. Many of them have for a long time sponsored testing programs for a variety of purposes. A survey conducted in 1967, for example, established that there were 74 state testing programs in 42 states, with 18 states offering two or more programs.[4] Most of those programs, however, were at that time intended principally for the guidance of students. Only 17 states were using tests to help evaluate instruction and only 13 to assess student progress. Most of the programs were not in any sense mandatory, nor did any of them provide information about the level and progress of education in the state as a whole. During the last four years there appears to have been a rising demand from state legislators, other state officials, and various public interest groups for this latter kind of information. Accompanied by various political overtones, the question is being asked more and more insistently: "How much and what kinds of measurable pupil learning and development is the state educational tax dollar buying?"

It is against this background that the present survey of state educational assessment programs was initiated in the fall of 1970. The survey has been a joint enterprise involving the Education Commission of the States, Educational Testing Service, and the ERIC Clearinghouse on Tests, Measurement, and Evaluation. The purpose of the survey was simply to find out as much as possible about what the states are planning and doing with regard to statewide educational assessment, what sorts of problems they are encountering in the process, and how they are coping with these problems. It is hoped that the information produced by this survey will help state education authorities achieve a better understanding of the possibilities open to them and the pitfalls to be avoided as they move into the assessment process.

The overall impression one gets from the survey is that state assessment plans and programs are currently in a highly fluid state, with new developments occurring daily. Accordingly, the facts and surmises presented in this report may well be out-of-date within a matter of months. It is for this reason that the entire survey should be viewed only as a snapshot of the situation existing early in the year of 1971. It is for this reason also that we hope this survey will be the first in a series by which, eventually, it will be possible to chart some trends.

In the next section of this overview we shall describe the procedures used in carrying out the survey. In the third section we shall discuss a number of major trends in the approach to state assessment that seem to be emerging. And in the last section we shall take a look at some of the more important problems that the states are encountering in their efforts.

II. The Survey Procedures

The goal of the survey was to obtain detailed information about educational assessment from all 50 states and the District of Columbia. The first step consisted of identifying in each state the two or three persons—usually officials in state education departments—who were most likely to be able to supply the needed information. The Education Commission of the States (ECS) assumed responsibility for assembling the list of state personnel to serve as contacts, for indicating to them the general purposes of the survey, and for enlisting their cooperation. Educational Testing Service (ETS) then assigned 21 persons from the professional staffs of its several field offices to conduct in-depth interviews with the state personnel identified by ECS.

The interviewing took place during the period from the middle of December to the first of March and on the average required about two days in each state. Each interviewer was furnished with an interview guide,[5] but each was also encouraged to go beyond the guide, as might be appropriate, in exploring the specific situation as he found it in the field. Accordingly, there is considerable variation in the nature of the interviewers' reports, and tidy statistics for comparing one state with another are lacking—not only because of the interviewers' differing perceptions of what they heard and saw, but also because of the many different ways in which the states are proceeding and the diverse rates at which they are developing their programs, if any.

There were, however, a number of points covered in practically all the interviews. All interviewers, for instance, inquired into the existence and nature of educational needs assessment programs and into what, if anything, was being done about setting educational goals for the state. They asked whether and to what extent lay citizens had been involved in formulating the goals and whether attempts had been made to translate broad goals into specific and measurable pupil performance objectives. Had advisory or policy commissions assisted in planning, and to what degree had assessment programs gone beyond the planning stage to the implementation of a pilot program or possibly one that was fully operational? Who had initiated the program—the state education department, the legislature, or some other agency inside or outside the state government? Was the control of the program centralized in a state agency, or was it dispersed to the local school districts, or to intermediate units?

Funding was another focus of inquiry. Had the legislature appropriated money especially for the purpose of educational assessment, or had the funds come from the federal government or from regular department budgets?

Technical support for assessment programs was also consistently investigated. Were the universities involved, regional educational laboratories, R and D Centers, private agencies?

Occasionally the states were asked two additional questions: 1) Were their programs being related to and assisted by the Federal-State Joint Task Force on Evaluation (the so-called "Belmont Project")?[6] And 2) Was the assessment program in any way involved with a statewide planning-programming-budgeting system?

Testing programs were examined in some detail. What types of measures, if any, were being used? What educational domains were being explored, and how? Were the measures norm-referenced or criterion-referenced? Were test score data being related to community and school factors? What students were touched by the program at what grade levels? Were all students in the selected grades involved or only a sample? Finally, who would share in the resulting test information? How would it be used? What was the climate in which the programs were conceived? How were the public and the profession responding to the effort? What were the political implications?

The reports submitted by the interviewers were in the form of discursive narratives. Each of these narratives was then summarized and sent back to the state agencies to be checked for accuracy. The summaries were then revised as needed.[7]

The writing of this overview chapter was sponsored by the ERIC Clearinghouse on Tests, Measurement, and Evaluation.

III. Major Trends in Approaches to Assessment

Although the educational assessment activities of the states are extremely varied, some similarities are immediately evident. One activity, for instance, that is universal is the mounting of educational needs assessment programs. Every state has conducted such a program, or is currently doing so, or is planning to recycle a completed one. The pervasiveness of this type of activity is readily explained by the fact that needs assessment is tied to receipt of ESEA, Title III funds, as specified in Section 402 of the act as amended.[8] Another activity involves more than half the states—27 at the present writing —in a joint effort to build the so-called Belmont System.[9] Formulating statewide educational goals is still another task in which many of the states are engaged. In this connection there seems to be increasing recognition that a comprehensive set of agreed-upon goals constitutes the essential defining characteristic of any fully developed educational assessment program—that is, one which can be distinguished from the piecemeal *ad hoc* testing programs of earlier decades. The way the goal-setting process is being conducted by many states represents one of the distinctly new trends picked up by the survey. We now turn our attention to this development.

The Setting of Statewide Educational Goals

The setting of educational goals by the states has been handled in different ways. Some states, for example, have updated broad goal statements adopted in the past, and they have attempted to translate them into measurable pupil performance objectives for each stage of schooling. A case in point is Colorado, which had adopted a set of educational goals in 1962 but never investigated the extent to which the goals were being achieved. Recently, however, as part of the statewide evaluation project now getting underway there, the Colorado Department of Education brought together a representative group of teachers and subject-matter specialists to specify measurable pupil-performance objectives corresponding to the 1962 goals, and, in a series of workshops at the University of Colorado, to develop tests for assessing progress toward each of the objectives. These tests have subsequently been administered on a pilot basis to students in a sample of schools throughout the state. Other states, not so far along in the goal-setting process, have been faced with the necessity of beginning the exercise *de novo*.

In addressing this problem, their approaches have varied. Some states are relying solely on professional educators for the establishment of statewide goals. Others, however, are also involving citizens from all walks of life in the exercise. The survey results suggest that the latter approach is becoming increasingly frequent.

From all accounts, however, bringing citizens and educators together for the purpose of discussing the ends of education can give rise to a process that is often unexpectedly arduous and time-consuming. The state of California, for example, has been going through this exercise for several years and anticipates that a few more years will be needed before the task can be completed. Its experience is illuminating.

Some time ago the California School Boards Association gathered statements of educational philosophy and goals from virtually every school district in the state. An analysis of the material from some 400 districts resulted in 18 definitions of basic goals. Although these 18 goal statements were given no official sanction by the state education authorities, the activity in and of itself has reportedly influenced state legislation, which now calls for the development of a common state curriculum, modified by local options, and which specifies further that the common curriculum shall be based upon some common set of goals and objectives agreed to in advance.

Concurrently with the work of the California School Boards Association, another group of citizens and educators was also concerning itself with the formulation of educational goals for California. This was the Advisory Committee on Achievement and Evaluation set up by the Education Committee of the California Assembly. After well over a year of hearings, the Advisory Committee recommended to the legislature that a state commission on educational goals and evaluation be established, and during the 1969 regular session a Joint Committee on Educational Goals and Evaluation was given a mandate to tackle the problem.

The Joint Committee, whose members are drawn from the Senate, the Assembly, and the State Board of Education, has appointed still another group of educators and citizens to form an Advisory Committee for Guidelines on Goals. Meantime, working with a staff of consultants, the Joint Committee has decided to require each school district to develop its own goals and objectives based upon the forthcoming guidelines. Ultimately these local goals are to be added to goals developed by the State Department of Education, by educational specialists, and by citizen advisors. Combined and edited, these goals and objectives will be submitted to the State Board of Education in 1973 together with an evaluation system designed to measure their attainment.

A different example of the apparently inevitable twists and turns that seem to accompany citizen participation in the goal-setting process is to be found in the "Our Schools" program in New Jersey. This program, which got underway in the spring of 1969, is being conducted under the aegis of a broadly representative group known as the Advisory Council on Educational Needs Assessment and is staffed by the Office of Planning in the State Department of Education.

The "Our Schools" program is attempting to answer four questions: 1) What do the citizens of New Jersey think their schools should be doing for the children and adults of the state? 2) How well are the schools of the state currently doing this job? That is, what are the gaps between goals and results? 3) What can be done in the next three to five years to close the gaps? 4) How can progress toward closing the gaps be measured?

Extensive citizen participation is a basic principle of the program. Two statewide conferences to draw up tentative goals were held in the spring of 1970, each involving about 100 representative laymen, professionals, and students. These were followed during the fall and winter of 1970-71 by 18 regional conferences, involving varying numbers of laymen and professionals, to rework the goals and help collect opinions on priorities. The outcomes of these regional conferences will be supplemented by additional conferences at the local district level and by a statewide poll of citizen opinions concerning public education. In the fall of 1971, the data generated by all this activity will be fed to a final statewide conference of about 300 persons who will attempt a final ordering of educational priorities for presentation to the State Board of Education. The Board will then have the responsibility of determining what the educational goals for the state as a whole are to be.

This mingling of laymen and professionals in the several states has occasioned a search for ways to do justice to large numbers of people and points of view and, at the same time, achieve a workable consensus within practical time limits. The survey reveals that some state educational agencies now plan to train their staffs in the use of the Delphi technique,[10] a process that may prove particularly useful in the goals-setting process. The Delphi technique was originally conceived as a way to obtain the opinions of experts without necessarily bringing them together face to face. The experts are consulted individually, as a rule by a series of questionnaires. Although there have been a number of adaptations, the general idea has been to prepare successive rounds of questions that elicit progressively more carefully considered group opinions. Experimentation has revealed that the process is able to produce a satisfactory degree of convergence of opinion.[11] To our knowledge, however, it has not yet been used with the very large numbers of persons and viewpoints such as those encountered, for instance, in the "Our Schools" program in New Jersey. If the trend toward community deliberation on state policy matters continues, there will need to be further adaptations of the Delphi technique in large-scale settings.

Assessment and Management Information Systems

In an earlier time, accounting systems in education were usually called upon for a fairly simple attesting that the public funds for education had been honestly administered. Such systems are now being asked increasingly to display relationships between the expenditures for school programs of various kinds and the benefits accruing from those programs in terms of student performance. As a result there is a notable trend in many states to apply to the management of the educational enterprise the principles of cost-benefit analysis embodied in some form of planning-programming-budgeting system

(PPBS) and to tie statewide educational assessment into such a system.[12]

Although progress toward the actual implementation of PPBS has been slow, this is not for want of enthusiasm among its proponents. The plain fact, however, is that many questions must still find answers before complete systems can be designed and confidently applied. For there is still much to be learned about how to isolate the costs of educational programs and about the analytical techniques for relating benefits to costs. Many state education departments are therefore planning to have their staffs trained in the skills requisite to developing and operating PPBS.

In New York State, for example, an adaptation of PPBS, Program Analysis and Review (PAR), is currently used by the State Education Department to help identify program problems, the main applications being the state's ESEA programs. In the future the Department plans to use information from its Basic Educational Data System (BEDS) in the PAR system to evaluate ESEA projects in terms of an input-process-output paradigm.

California has similarly been developing PPBS for several years. The system has already been pilot tested and subsequently revised and retested. Although PPBS is not yet mandated for the entire state school system, reports are that it is likely to be authorized by the legislature and be fully operational by 1973-74.

Hawaii's legislature has recently called upon the State Department of Education to undertake the same kind of effort, since it is eager for data on educational results and is expecting that the new system will furnish the desired information on how well education in the state is faring relative to the amount of money being spent on it. The Department plans to feed into the system data from its well-established state testing program.

The Federal-State Joint Task Force on Evaluation (Belmont System) may be having a not unrelated impact on the development of state educational management control systems. As noted before, 27 states are now participants in the project's many activities, which at present also include the development of a Management Assessment System for state education agencies and its testing in a few states. It is possible that the kind of thinking and training required for this and related Belmont activities may have a spillover effect on developing rationales and methodologies for statewide assessment systems.

The Belmont group is not only concerned with building instruments for collecting a broad range of information on the nature, cost, and effectiveness of many kinds of educational programs in school districts; it is also concerned, perhaps more importantly, with the development of methods for training state and local personnel in the use of these instruments. As a consequence, Belmont may be seen as a comprehensive effort to bring into being an information system that can possibly have just as much usefulness in the management of state and local educational programs as it may have for federally supported programs.

Assessment and Statewide Testing Programs

Although educational assessment, properly viewed, involves a good deal more than statewide testing programs, testing seems, nevertheless, to be looming larger and larger in the plans for assessment. In fact, many of the authorizations from legislatures are principally for the assessment of education by tests. That is, there is a mounting legislative pressure for documenting the products of the educational process by statewide testing programs. Some states have already set in motion widely ranging programs of tests (Pennsylvania and Michigan being notable examples), and others report themselves to be at the point of doing so (among them Colorado and Delaware). Some states are starting with rather narrow content coverage, but are planning for massive programs later on (Florida and Georgia, for example).

The content of most current state testing programs—whether mandated or unmandated by legislative bodies—is often less surprising than it is significant. The states engaged in some form of assessment-by-testing are mainly concerned with how well their educational systems are succeeding in imparting basic skills. Only a relatively few go beyond the three R's to get information on how education is affecting student values and attitudes. Arizona, for example, received a mandate for the Arizona State Third Grade Reading Achievement Program, to begin this year. Although the specific objectives of the program are not yet available, strong effort will apparently be made to provide background data to lend depth and perspective in interpreting test scores.

As another example, recent legislation in Michigan calls for measures of the basic skills at grades 4 and 7. This program, which is now in its second year, covers verbal analogies, reading, English (mechanics of written English), and mathematics. In the first year, only average scores by school and school district were reported, since the tests were consciously designed to be too short to yield adequately reliable scores on individual students. This approach, however, was changed for the 1970-71 administrations. Tests are now of conventional length to provide the schools with information concerning the achievement of individuals. Although the major stress here has been on the academic areas, the Michigan program has also given some attention to assessing the influence of schooling on student aspirations.

California, which has a history of mandated testing programs going back to 1961, is another instance where testing of the basic skills has been strongly emphasized. In 1965, the Miller-Unruh Basic Reading Act created an obligatory testing program in reading for the primary grades. This concentration on the basics has been further reinforced by a recent legislative requirement for the adoption of minimum academic standards for certain grades and the selection of tests to be used statewide in evaluating the attainment of these standards.

Delaware is one of the states that is starting small. It is currently testing achievement and mental ability in all schools, but at the fifth grade only. It is looking ahead, however, to a program that will include all students in all grades, K through 12, in all schools, public and private. Program development in other states is following a similar pattern. Florida, for example, is presently concerned with measuring only achievement in reading, but under legislative prodding is also planning a most ambitious program that will sample students in kindergarten through grade 12 in all the basic subjects.

Assessment of Noncognitive Development

Although the principal intent of most state testing programs is to get a reading on the cognitive development of students, a few states make a point of stressing additionally the importance of personal-social development as an outcome of the educational process. Thus, the idea that education is to be construed simply as a process for inculcating the fundamental cognitive skills no longer totally dominates educational thought and practice.

In recognition of the importance to the student and society of noncognitive development, Pennsylvania includes in its targets for quality education a number of attitudes and noncognitive abilities that it wishes its public schools to nurture. Consequently, the state educational agency has produced instruments to gauge how extensively schools are affecting such significant aspects of human life as self-concept, understanding of others, responsible citizenship, health habits, creativity, the acquisition of salable skills, the understanding of human accomplishments, readiness for change, and students' attitudes toward their schools. Michigan, too, has included in its testing program the measurement of three types of student attitudes: namely, attitude toward learning, attitude toward academic achievement, and attitude toward self. Nebraska is now planning to create an assessment program which, in its first stage, will be concerned *only* with nonacademic objectives.

Measuring the Influences on Learning

A fifth trend, and a significant advance in mounting state testing programs, is the commitment on the part of a number of states to assessing the outcomes of education only after accounting for the effects of community and home environment, of teachers and school programs, and of school facilities and financial resources. To judge from the planning reported in the survey, this is a development in the assessment process that presumably will grow in importance, especially if the Belmont System continues to expand its services and refine its battery of instruments. For example, the most recent plans of the Belmont group are "to demonstrate now that the System can provide meaningful inputs to the State and/or local educational agencies to assist them in the performance of their basic program functions. This can be partially accomplished through development of a model for a State Data Analysis Plan. Such a model would be designed to indicate the potential uses of Belmont System data in relation to existing state and local data resources and would tie these together as input to the continuing program evaluation required at both State and local levels to meet the information and decision-making needs of program managers at these levels . . ."[13]

The Belmont group expects to begin this year to study total state assessment needs. In fact, some of the group's instruments, now being developed, may be of direct service to any state wishing to assess the influence on its schools of input and process factors. Questionnaires have been constructed to elicit information on organization patterns in schools, the training of personnel, programs and services, condition of school facilities, size and location of school, nature and size of staff, and the like. Other instruments supply information that can provide the basis for evaluating program effectiveness, as, for example, data on classroom facilities, classroom organization, programs of instruction, teacher background, and pupil's grade, age, sex, absences, background characteristics, academic program participation, behavior, and performance.

Among current statewide programs, Michigan's, for example, relates all achievement measures to student and school characteristics. Each student anonymously supplies information from which socioeconomic status and aspiration scales are derived. Records maintained in the State Department of Education provide school and district information such as teacher/pupil ratio, financial resources per student, average teacher experience, and location by type of community. Similarly, the program in Pennsylvania attempts to measure input variables of three major types, which include 8 having to do with the student's background, 4 having to do with the community in which the school is located, and 27 that have to do with school staff characteristics. Community conditions are derived from a Student Information Form. Norms have been developed by the Pennsylvania Educational Quality Assessment, so that school districts can compare pupil achievements, taking into account socioeconomic and other differences in pupils, schools, and communities.

These comprehensive approaches to the assessment of the educational process, school by school, are still relatively rare. However, more and more states appear to be getting interested in the possibility of going in the same direction.

Influence of the National Assessment Model

The survey reveals that, as states tool up for assessment, they are considering whether to use some kind of sampling approach—that is, to obtain information from a relatively small but representative group of students located in representative regions and types of communities in the state—or to use an "every-pupil" approach. Settling the issue often appears to depend on how the purpose of statewide assessment is locally perceived.

If the state wishes principally to supply its decisionmakers with satisfactory information about the level and progress of the state's educational system as a whole, the sampling approach is regarded as sufficient. In this connection, the survey reveals a rather pervasive influence of the National Assessment model on state assessment designs. This model is based on matrix sampling techniques and randomization in the packaging of test exercises. Under this strategy, only a few pupils in each school or school district try a few test items drawn from very large pools of items.[14] The model is reportedly attractive because it does not subject any pupil to many hours of testing, while at the same time it provides a large quantity of information on what various segments of the student population are learning during the school years. Colorado and Florida are two states whose plans are based on this kind of sampling approach.

If, on the other hand, the state wishes to couple management-oriented results with information that can be returned to each school for self-appraisal and for the guidance of students, then the every-pupil approach is clearly the appropriate alternative. Georgia's plans at present envision this approach.

These, of course, are not the only possibilities open to the states. There are plans and programs that adopt the "whole-test" approach while testing only a sample of the children in selected grades at any given time.

The evidence is not yet clear enough for a prediction of which sampling patterns will ultimately predominate. As programs move past discussion-and-drawing-board stages, future surveys should illuminate further and document the various conditions and considerations that influence choices.

The Control of Assessment Programs

The control of state educational assessment programs follows several patterns. In some states there is a strong tendency toward the centralization of control in the state department of education. In others the tendency is to vest much of the control in the local school districts. In still others, there is a kind of balanced tension between the two tendencies. Nevertheless, the results of the survey suggest that, insofar as testing is a component of assessment, there may be a slight trend toward more centralized control of the assessment process, even in those cases where participation in the program is optional with the local education authorities. In such cases the state authority assumes responsibility for specifying the purpose, content, and target populations of the programs, but the local districts may be left free to accept or reject the state's services. At the same time, however, there is a noticeable if small increase in programs whose results are aggregated and analyzed for the entire state and reported by a central agency to legislatures or to state boards of education as well as back to the administrators of the local school districts. This naturally occurs where legislation so stipulates.

The survey also indicates that where some form of centralized operating control exists, the state department of education is not necessarily the agency that exercises it. Indeed, the control may be based in the education department of a state university or, as is the case currently in Texas, in regional centers that have been established by law but which work largely independently of the state department of education.

Thus, local programs of assessment and local options to participate in centralized programs continue unchanged as typical manifestations of the folkways of American education. Yet the survey gives some salience to procedures that begin to combine, in novel and even ingenious ways, the two approaches to control. That is, as the states feel constrained to renew or to rationalize their educational systems, some have adopted models to permit both maximum feasible local autonomy *and* the exercise of state leadership in improving local educational processes. An interesting instance is the Vermont Design for Education. The emphasis here is on the *state's* requiring an extraordinary degree of *local* involvement in educational planning. In effect, Vermont has required each locality to build its own locally created design for education and has also required full citizen involvement in setting goals and priorities. The Vermont Design was created by the state education agency.[15] Its purpose, however, was not to impose programs, but to stimulate vision, discussion, and creativity. This "conversation-piece" model also includes state-developed instruments that the districts are free to use if they wish—or to adapt or reject in favor of locally devised tests and other measures. The state agency also stands ready to offer assistance when the locality is in need of technical expertise. A representative of the Vermont State Department of Education, for example, sits in on community meetings as a source of immediate technical assistance and information. Hence, although there is direct influence, there are no constraints on the form and shape of local programs. The central agency's effect is to lead autonomous localities in the direction of self-determined innovation. The state commissioner will receive formal reports of the resultant programs, but they will not be publicized.

IV. Some Emerging Problems

Embedded in all this state assessment activity we detect a variety of problems emerging which, in our view, will need more attention than they have generally been getting if much of the planning now underway is not to be frustrated. These problems have to do largely with the strategies and tactics by which viable programs of assessment are to be brought into being and maintained. The problems fall into four categories: 1) lack of communication and coordination, 2) the relation of assessment data to financial incentives, 3) the handling of sensitive data, and 4) confusion and conflict about goals.

The Problem of Coordination and Communication

In some states a number of different groups appear to be going their separate ways in moving toward the design of some sort of educational assessment program. These disparate groups may include legislative committees, citizen committees (self-appointed or governor-appointed), state boards of education, state departments of education, and even different segments of the bureaucracy within a state department. The absence of any serious effort to coordinate the efforts of these several groups or to open up lines of communication among them can generate conflict and confusion which threaten to neutralize the entire enterprise.

There is, for example, the recent case of a legislature that adopted two conflicting statutes whereby some of the well-laid plans for one statewide testing program were effectively nullified by the legal specifications for a second program.

In another state three programs appear to be moving independently along nonconvergent parallel lines toward the same ultimate objective. One program under the control of one branch of the department of education is trying to develop a statewide consensus on educational goals; another under the control of a committee of the legislature is trying to develop a state-aid system that will include a requirement that each local school district devise its own appropriate goals; and a third under the control of another branch of the department of education is looking toward a statewide evaluation program based upon a set of goals not yet determined.

In yet another state at least four different programs, each under separate auspices and each separately staffed, are in various stages of development. One of these is being developed by a governor-appointed commission which is looking into school financing and assessment programs that might be devised to rationalize the process. A second, located in one of the divisions of the state department of education, has been providing, on an optional basis for a number of years, a battery of tests and other measures whereby a school system may, if it wishes, assess the effectiveness of its instructional programs. A third, operated by another division of the same department, administers a statewide testing program on a required basis to all elementary schools in the state and provides its own advisory services to help school personnel use the results to evaluate educational progress by comparison with state norms. Finally, still another branch of the department, using different data, has been working for several years on checking out the feasibility of an input-output model for measuring school effectiveness.

Diversity in the efforts to build an educational assessment system for a state is probably inevitable as a consequence of professional and political rivalries among the several groups concerned. It can be argued that such diversity in some amount is desirable in that it may help to ensure that a system best adapted to the state's needs will eventually emerge.

On the other hand, when fragmentation of the planning activities becomes so extreme that there is little if any communication among the planners, the whole effort can be counterproductive in at least two ways. It can create so much confusion in the local school districts that they will tend to sabotage any and all assessment programs that may be forthcoming. And it can result in so much duplication of effort as to be wasteful of time, money, and the technical expertise that is still extremely scarce.

Accordingly, if state educational assessment is to fulfill its very real promise as an instrument for helping educational systems upgrade the quality of their services, it would appear that means must be found for exchanging ideas about what a sound assessment program in a given state might be and for encouraging cooperation among those involved in the development of programs.

The Relation of Assessment Data to Financial Incentives

Another problem beginning to crop up where statewide assessment programs are actually underway has to do with the manner in which the results will be used in allocating state funds to local school districts. One can put the problem in the form of four questions:

1) Does one use the funds to reward the districts that show up high on the indicators?
2) Does one withhold the funds to punish the districts that show up low on the indicators?
3) Does one use the funds to help upgrade the districts that show up low on the indicators and thereby withhold funds from those that show up high?
4) Or can one find a way to allocate the funds so that all districts will have an incentive for constantly improving the quality of their schools?

These are agonizing questions that have apparently not been adequately thought through. For example, one state is now using reading test scores in a formula for determining the specific sums of money that will be allocated to school districts to provide reading specialist teachers. Depending on the progress of the students, the school can suddenly find itself without funds for specialized assistance because it has previously been successful in improving reading levels.

In another state—where there is similar legislation—funds are being awarded to schools that rank lowest on common measures. Some school principals who are serious about their responsibilities are beginning to talk of deliberately over-speeding test administrations so that school performance as measured by the tests will *not* come up to the mark. Their reasoning apparently is that if failure is to be rewarded, then it is folly to be successful.

Sound answers must be found to these questions. If they are not, the whole assessment enterprise runs the risk of provoking the outrage of both the public and the professional educators.

The Handling of Sensitive Data

One particularly troubling problem beginning to surface has to do with the confidentiality of information supplied by pupils, teachers, and others who may be involved in some aspect of the assessment process. The question arises in the first instance in connection with the release of achievement test scores of individual pupils and the averages of such scores, class by class, or school by school, or even, in some cases, district by district. The fear is that data of this sort will be misinterpreted by the public and be used to make unwarranted and invidious comparisons.

The problem is further exacerbated when pupils and/or their teachers are asked to supply information about their ethnicity, their economic and social backgrounds, their behavior tendencies, and their social attitudes. Hard questions are raised not only concerning the propriety of using such information once it is in hand, but also concerning the possible deleterious effects on children of merely asking for such information in the first place. It is argued, with some cogency, for instance, that to ask a child from a broken home "Who acts as your father?" can be psychologically damaging to the child; it can also be regarded as invading privacy.

Furthermore, there is always the doubt whether the responses to such questions can be taken at face value as a true representation of the child's home conditions. Similarly, in respect to questions about attitudes, the doubt is always present whether the respondent may be "faking good" or "faking bad" and not representing his true feelings about himself and others.

As a consequence, any comprehensive assessment program that attempts to secure data on the many interacting variables bearing upon the multiple outcomes of the educational process is confronted with a serious dilemma. Unless the kinds of sensitive data suggested above become available, any assessment of what schools are doing to and for students will be less than complete and very likely misleading. On the other hand, the ethical and practical difficulties in collecting such data are very real difficulties that are not easily overcome.

Recently, for example, some schools involved in a state testing program refused to return the students' answer sheets on the ground that the responses they contained might be used to penalize the individual student because of his background or possibly to impugn the reputation of his ethnic group. And this reaction occurred despite the fact that the information was gathered in a manner that guaranteed the anonymity of the suppliers thereof and despite the announced intent to use the information only for the purpose of assessing the overall impact of educational programs on each of several target populations of students. In short, even though the state authority may be doing its best to protect the integrity of the data required for giving the public a reasonably accurate picture of the educational benefits its tax dollars are buying, the public in turn is often so dubious of the credibility of the state authority in these matters that efforts to develop sound assessment procedures are in danger of reaching an impasse.

Some attempts have been made to circumvent the sensitivity-of-data problem by relying on various types of "social indicators." This is done by using existing data collections—for example, federal, state, and local statistical reports on community economic status, health, juvenile delinquency rates, the use of public libraries, concert halls, museums, and the like. Each such indicator is presumed to be capable of giving some indirect information relative to the overall impact of schooling on children. However, the difficulty with these kinds of indicators of school effects is well known and far from being dispelled.[16] The difficulty inheres in their very indirectness, in the fact that the level of such indices is determined by many social and community factors beyond the reach of the schools.[17] Hence, they are highly vulnerable to misinterpretation.

Confusions and Conflicts about Goals

In the various efforts to formulate meaningful goals upon which to build assessment programs, there appears to be a considerable amount of confusion between the ends and means of education, between process and product, between inputs and outputs, and between pupil performance objectives, staff objectives, and system objectives. This sort of confusion pervades not only public discussions of educational goals; it appears to be just as rife in the deliberations of the professional educators themselves.

The following list of abbreviated goal statements is not unrepresentative of the kind of mix such discussions frequently produce:

To help students become effective participants in society

To increase the ratio of guidance counselors to pupils

To ensure that students acquire sound health habits

To ensure that all students are capable of reading "at grade level"

To reward teaching and administrative personnel in accordance with the degree to which they produce learning in students

To reduce class size by increasing the ratio of teachers to pupils

To provide more effective in-service training for school personnel

To ensure that every student shall have acquired a marketable skill by the time he or she graduates from high school

To stimulate community involvement in the work of the schools

To reduce the student dropout rate

To modernize and enlarge school facilities

To give students a sense of their worth as human beings

To keep school budgets as low as possible consistent with sound education

To sensitize teachers to the individual learning needs of the children they teach

To bring the results of research to bear on the actual operations of the schools

To promote better understanding among ethnic, racial, and economic groups

The difficulty with such an indiscriminate collection lies in the fact that the individual goal statements, however worthy in themselves, are so diverse in type that there is no way to compare them with one another and thereby arrive at priorities among them. Some attempts have been made to get around this difficulty by sorting the goals into homogeneous categories of objectives, such as societal objectives, pupil performance objectives, process objectives, staff requirement objectives, financial objectives, and the like. Even so, however, the vexing problem of how to work out the probable *interrelationships* among the several categories has seldom been addressed in any explicit way. Nor, despite the efforts of system analysts to develop the necessary conceptual schemes and procedures for rationalizing the relationships, does there appear to be much inclination among educational policy makers and practitioners to come to grips with the problem.

One reason for this state of affairs seems to lie in the very real complexity of the goal-making process. It is no mean task to sort out, even in rough fashion, the several types of goals, to make them operational in terms of defining measures, and to visualize the possible relationships among all the interacting variables. As a consequence, goal making tends to become an exercise in rhetoric, seen by many as simply a way of postponing if not avoiding hard decisions about such matters as the level of financial support for the schools, the method of allocating funds, the bases for hiring and firing teachers, the scope of services the schools are to provide, and the like.

A second reason for the confusion about goals seems to lie in the conflicting interests among and within the many different groups having a direct economic and/or political stake in the educational enterprise—parents, taxpayers, teachers, school executives, school board members, legislators, bureaucrats, commercial suppliers of plant and equipment, and, not least, the students themselves. The questions that inevitably trouble the members of these groups are: "What is there in it for me? Are the goals on which an educational assessment program is to be based consistent with my own goals? And to what extent will the program be a threat to my attainment of them?"

These are questions that must be squarely faced and coped with by educational leaders and planners if statewide assessment is to fulfill its promise. Somehow the numerous constituencies in the vast social undertaking we call education must be helped to understand that they have a *common* stake in the process, that educational assessment, when properly conceived and conducted, has the overriding purpose of increasing knowledge about what is effective in education, deepening understanding of all aspects of the educational process, opening education to all the publics concerned, and extending the ability of the schools to meet the diverse developmental needs of all students of all ages and conditions.

It is our hope that future surveys of statewide educational assessment programs will extend information on how all these problems are being dealt with so as to assist the planners-to-come in evaluating available strategies for making assessment an effective means of improving the benefits of education through informed decision making in all parts of the system.

Notes

1. Ralph W. Tyler, "Assessing the Progress of Education," *Phi Delta Kappan* 47 (September 1965), 13-16. For a recent description of the National Assessment Program in operation, see F. B. Womer, *What is National Assessment* (Ann Arbor, Mich.: National Assessment of Educational Progress, 1970).

2. Public Law 89-10, 89th Congress, H.R. 2362, April 11, 1965, Sec. 205 (a)(5).

3. J. S. Coleman *et al.*, *Equality of Educational Opportunity* (Washington, D.C.: U.S. Government Printing Office, 1966).

4. Educational Testing Service, *State Testing Programs: A Survey of Functions, Tests, Materials and Services* (Princeton, N.J.: Educational Testing Service, 1968).

5. Educational Testing Service, *Interview Guide: Survey of Statewide Educational Assessment Programs, 1971.*

6. U.S. Office of Education, *Federal/State Task Force on Educational Evaluation: An Overview* (Washington, D.C.: the Task Force, 1971).

7. The state-by-state summaries are presented in the full report by Dyer and Rosenthal, *State Educational Assessment Programs* (Princeton, N.J.: Educational Testing Service, 1971).

8. Public Law 90-247, 90th Congress, H.R. 7819, January 2, 1968, Sec. 402.

9. The Council of Chief State School Officers and the U.S. Office of Education in 1968 jointly agreed to develop and implement a comprehensive educational evaluation system in an effort to consolidate state reporting of the several federal programs as required by law. The initial meetings took place at the Belmont House in Elkridge, Maryland, and the program has become known as the "Belmont Project." Planned for eventual use in all states, the program presently includes 27 pilot states. Representatives of these states, together with USOE personnel, comprise a Task Force responsible for general development and direction of the project. All states are tied into the project through Evaluation Coordinators appointed by their chiefs.

10. W. T. Weaver, "The Delphi Forecasting Method," *Phi Delta Kappan* 52 (January 1971), 52, 267-71.

11. N. P. Uhl, *Encouraging Convergence of Opinion, through the Use of the Delphi Technique, in the Process of Identifying an Institution's Goals* (Princeton, N.J.: Educational Testing Service, 1971).

12. W. H. Curtis, *Project to Develop a Program Planning-Budgeting-Evaluation System Design: First Year Final Progress Report* (Chicago: Research Corporation of the Association of School Business Officials, 1968).

13. *Federal/State Task Force on Educational Evaluation: An Overview*, 29.

14. F. M. Lord, "Estimating Norms by Item-Sampling," *Educational and Psychological Measurement* 22 (Summer 1962), 259-67. This paper contains one of the earliest investigations of the possibilities in item-sampling for estimating the parameters of test-score distributions. This technique set the stage for what is now known as matrix sampling. See also F. M. Lord and M. Novick, *Statistical Theories of Mental Test Scores* (Reading, Mass.: Addison-Wesley, 1968), ch. 11.

15. The Vermont Department of Education, *Vermont Design for Education* (Montpelier: Vermont Department of Education, 1969).

16. R. A. Bauer (ed.), *Social Indicators* (Cambridge, Mass.: Massachusetts Institute of Technology Press, 1966).

17. U. S. Department of Health, Education, and Welfare, *Toward A Social Report* (Ann Arbor, Mich.: University of Michigan Press, 1970).

Some Current State Assessment Programs

National Assessment of Educational Progress

At least 14 states are adding a new dimension to evaluations of their schools: ability to compare student achievement results with national and regional data and to spot curriculum weaknesses by using NAEP materials.

By using some of the same exercises and survey techniques pioneered by NAEP, states can obtain educational assessment results comparable with those obtained on a regional and national basis by NAEP, said J. Stanley Ahmann, NAEP staff director. And a swiftly increasing number of states are using, or exploring, the idea.

Actually, state educational officials find NAEP-type data useful in two ways, Ahmann said.

First, state assessments with nationwide or regional comparability give educational decision makers new insights into areas of strength and weakness in school programs.

Second, NAEP-type assessment results, because they describe student achievement in terms of concrete items of knowledge, can give the public a clear idea of what students are learning. This helps in an era when both the public and state legislators are holding school systems accountable for results to match time and money invested.

The state of Maine released its first results in November—findings based on an educational assessment program closely paralleling that of NAEP. In 1972, the Maine State Department of Education conducted an assessment of citizenship knowledge and writing skills among 17-year-olds in both public and private schools.

In citizenship, results indicate a tendency for Maine young people to surpass the national performance on concern for the well-being of others, and for their rights as individuals. Maine officials pointed out, however, that national achievement was so low in some of these areas that "Maine should not take comfort."

This review of current educational assessment activities at the state level appeared in the *Newsletter* of the National Assessment of Educational Progress, 6 (February 1973). It is reprinted here with permission of the Editor of the *Newsletter*.

"Results indicate that a better understanding of constitutional freedoms as they apply to real life, and the development of practical skills in citizen participation in government, are two areas of civic education in which we must increase our effectiveness as educators," said Carroll R. McGary, commissioner of the Maine State Department of Educational and Cultural Services.

This assessment, according to Joe Natale, project director, is part of a 10-year program planned to give Maine not only data on current student performance but also comparable data on changes in performance over time.

"The quality of the NAEP methodology, the project's exploration of children's understandings, feelings, and skills provides salient information in light of the public demand for education progress data. We anticipate that our curriculum people will do further analysis of the data and that program planning will be based in part on the results of our assessment," Natale added.

Other states which have already included various NAEP components in their assessment programs include Connecticut, Massachusetts, Colorado, and Iowa.

Connecticut conducted a statewide assessment of reading performance using a selection of NAEP exercises. Results were released in September 1972.

Although overall performance for 9-, 13- and 17-year-olds was consistently higher than the national percentage of people giving correct responses, the large city group was below the national large city performance in the four skills assessed: understanding, analysis, judgment, and use of printed materials.

The largest differences were apparent among 9-year-olds. Those from small towns were 13.8 percent above the national results in small towns in analyzing what they had read. Those from the large cities were 15.3 percent below the results for large cities in making judgments about what they had read.

Connecticut, after reviewing the results, is now acting to improve the reading programs in its five largest cities. The first step of a plan proposed by the Connecticut State Department of Education is a study to determine the types of reading programs now used in the schools of the five largest cities and the types of state and federal funds being used in the programs.

William J. Sanders, Connecticut state education commissioner, as quoted in the New York *Times,* said the data collected in the assessment "will provide bases for the further development of reading curricula, the professional education of teachers and the more effective use of available educational resources."

Massachusetts, in statewide sampling of 7th grade students' performance in science and citizenship, used NAEP exercises, among others, with scoring and analysis done according to NAEP criteria.

In this state, however, scores were not compared with NAEP national and regional results. Massachusetts results were reported in terms of how much public and nonpublic school students knew about the items covered in the exercises. And the exercises were chosen in accordance with educational priorities suggested by a sampling of 7th grade teachers.

This, according to NAEP officials, illustrates a feature of NAEP assessment that state officials find attractive. They can use as much or as little of the NAEP materials and methods as they wish. They can choose only exercises based on educational objectives compatible with NAEP national or regional baselines or not, as they choose.

"What has been achieved is an increased interest and endorsement by Massachusetts educators of mastery level testing," said James F. Baker, associate commissioner for research, planning, and evaluation in the Massachusetts State Department of Education. It was the first time many educators looked at test evaluation data in terms of their relationship to curriculum, and their acceptance of it is a step forward, he said.

Baker sees a need for a greater amount of such data in order to make sound educational decisions affecting the entire curriculum. However, he said, "we feel we successfully demonstrated an important process in which local school districts had involvement."

By March, Massachusetts teachers will have ranked objectives in reading for grades 2 through 9 and in mathematics for grades 1 through 12. Mastery level testing in these areas will be done before the end of the year.

Colorado conducted a science assessment in the spring of 1972 borrowing from NAEP objectives and exercises and following the NAEP sampling method.

Colorado students, on the average, ranged from 7 percent above to 5 percent below the national percentage of people giving correct answers on 13 science items that were compared. Results on the total test, which included these 13 items, were reported for the state and each participating district.

Results are used by the state to guide Title III funding and by districts for purposes of accountability and measurement of their individual programs.

John Helper, consultant with the Colorado State Department of Education, said, "Colorado has relied a great deal on National Assessment materials and procedures in developing state plans and intends to make further use, concentrating on actual use of these results for state and local decisions." In the spring of 1973, Colorado plans to assess mathematics, reading, and language arts.

NAEP objectives and exercises are being used by the Iowa Department of Public Instruction. "The division's efforts are directed to assist schools in developing models and strategies to assess their own educational needs, and National Assessment materials will be an integral part of these efforts," said David Alvord, consultant in the division of planning, research, and evaluation.

In 1971, Iowa administered the released NAEP science exercises to a state sample of students in grades 4, 7, and 12. A comparison of Iowa assessment results with results for the central region of the nation shows that Iowa student performance was, in general, equal or above student performance in the central region.

In 1972, Iowa administered appropriate NAEP reading and literature exercises to a similar sample and conducted a verification study of NAEP objectives to determine their importance in Iowa.

Results for reading for grades 4, 7, and 12 should be available this month. No comparison to national is made. "Instead, results will be analyzed on the basis of whether or not objectives that exercises were designed to measure are in fact being met," Alvord said.

Estimated difficulty levels, defined by NAEP, will be used as a basis for judging the success of Iowa students. "In this way," Alvord said, "we hope to find the kinds of things students are having difficulty with and from there change the curriculum to meet these needs."

Reading objectives will be made available to districts for local assessments.

Other states consulting with NAEP as they develop assessment programs include: Maryland, Louisiana, Wyoming, Minnesota, Illinois, Missouri, Arizona, Wisconsin, and Alabama.

Montgomery County, Md. is extending the NAEP system to the school district level. It will use NAEP materials and procedures this school year to assess writing skills of 13- and 17-year-old students. Maryland is using this as a pilot project to determine the adaptibility of NAEP methodology to both state and local educational levels.

Louisiana plans to conduct a reading assessment similar to Connecticut's this spring. It will use some different NAEP exercises which better match the state's objectives and will also add some locally developed exercises to measure some objectives more completely than NAEP.

Some NAEP exercises and procedures will be used in the Wyoming Educational Needs Assessment Project (WYENAP), which is now developing its measurement tools and conducting pilot tests. The project has outlined its assessment program through 1977 and will use NAEP materials and state-developed exercises in areas not covered by NAEP such as physical education, health, and foreign languages.

In the fall of 1973, WYENAP will conduct an assessment of writing, science, literature, and reading borrowing from NAEP for assessment of the cognitive areas of learning and developing on their own materials to assess the affective and psychomotor areas.

"Through the NAEP Department of Utilization/Applications we have received a tremendous amount of assistance in utilizing National Assessment materials and modifying them for our own assessment," James Headlee, director of the project, said.

The Minnesota State Department of Education is preparing a report on its assessment in reading and math conducted during 1971-72 using a state developed model. The assessment, a pilot study to develop an assessment model, involved 3rd and 6th grade students.

"After experience with a state developmental effort, we would like to use National Assessment methods, materials, and technology because the National Assessment results give meaningful references for state results," John Adams, director of statewide educational assessment, said.

Great pains have been taken to develop the NAEP model and Minnesota would have to undertake extensive effort to develop similar materials, he said. "National Assessment has a high quality, well-conceived model that offers much to state assessments," Adams added.

The Illinois State Department of Public Instruction used a series of public hearings to heavily involve citizens in establishing state educational goals which were published in May 1972. Illinois is now "studying alternative methods for collecting information to provide information about how well students are attaining the goals," according to Thomas Springer, director of assessment. "We are involving a group of educators to develop objectives prior to selecting exercises to measure the attainment. One of the major alternatives is National Assessment, including the model, objectives, and exercises," he said.

The Missouri State Department of Education has adopted the NAEP model for development and implementation of its long-range assessment plan.

Four main education goals have been adopted by the state board of education: intellectual, physical, social, and career development. During the fall of 1972, committees composed of education staff, local school district personnel, and college and university staff developed sets of NAEP-type education objectives in 17 interdisciplinary areas related to these four goals (i.e., qualitative thinking, scientific understanding, health, cultural awareness).

These objectives are now being reviewed by the local school districts through committees of teachers, students, and laymen. Development of exercises will begin in the summer of 1974, and the assessment will be administered in the spring of 1975.

"The Missouri assessment plan calls for the collection of statewide data through matrix sampling techniques at several grade levels," John Allan, chairman of the assessment project, said.

Arizona is involved in setting up objectives for a science assessment planned for early spring. Science teachers, department heads, and other science professionals are using NAEP objectives as a base for developing state objectives.

William Raymond, director of planning and evaluation, Arizona State Department of Education, said the plans thus far would involve students in grades 8 and 11. The Arizona Needs Assessment Committee will review the assessment plans for approval.

Wisconsin will assess reading capabilities of 3rd and 7th grade students in the spring. They are adopting NAEP testing approaches based on NAEP objectives. In addition to objectives-based exercises, they will use the "cloze" reading test developed by John Bormuth of the University of Chicago.

"We realize the desirability of using the objectives-based approach to assessment because such information can be directly related to determining the adequacy of instructional programs," said Jack Schmidt, director of the state assessment program, Wisconsin Department of Public Instruction. And the purpose of the assessment is to objectively determine educational needs in the state of Wisconsin, he said.

Alabama is planning an objectives-based assessment. The state is now identifying goals through various sources: graduates of the last four years, dropouts who left school at the beginning of senior high, parents, teachers, and upper-level students.

As the goals become more definitive and learning needs are identified, subject areas for the assessment will be determined by teachers. "The development of exercises will involve use of National Assessment materials," said F. L. Temple, chairman of supervision and curriculum development in the college of education at the University of Alabama.

The assessment involves two local school districts. Once the model is developed, it will be disseminated by the state in other school districts and possibly adopted for state use, Temple said.

11. Assessing Education at the Local Level

Richard M. Wolf

It is not possible to predict what the character of assessment programs at the local level will be. However, a historical examination of the role of measurement in education can be suggestive of some of the ingredients of such programs. While the first use of uniform written examinations in schools in the United States is usually attributed to Horace Mann in 1846, credit is usually given to Dr. J. M. Rice as being the "real inventor of the comparative test" in America in 1894.[1] Rice had developed a series of spelling tests which he used in a major study of the relationship between the amount of time devoted to spelling instruction and spelling achievement. Shortly after the turn of the century, E. L. Thorndike turned his attention to the field of testing, and he and his students were directly responsible for most of the early standard tests and scales for measuring achievement as well as for a number of highly influential publications on statistical methods in education and pioneer work on intelligence tests for college entrance. At about the same time, a series of studies on the unreliability of school marks and essay examinations began to appear, which convincingly demonstrated that school marks were highly subjective—the mark often being more a function of the person doing the marking than the performance of the student.

The reaction to such subjectivity led to a demand for more objective methods of appraising student performance. The initial success of the tests and scales developed by Thorndike and his students and the appearance of the Stanford-Binet intelligence test, which showed that scores on this test correlated well with ability to do school work, convinced many people that the solution to the problems of assessment in American education lay in the adoption of objective measures of performance. The years from about 1915 to 1930 have frequently been referred to as the "boom" period in American testing. Many objective tests designed to measure academic skills and various content areas of the school program were developed and marketed with great enthusiasm. Tests of intelligence and achievement were administered widely and often indiscriminately. Test results were often uncritically accepted and served as the basis for a variety of judgments and actions with respect to individuals and programs. If only tests were objective, it was felt, they were assumed to be sufficiently accurate for valid comparisons, not only of one class or school with another, but also of one pupil with another.

Reaction to widespread and often uncritical use of tests began to emerge around 1930. Specific criticisms made of tests and the use of test results included the use of test scores as a basis for classroom grouping, the limited scope of many tests as well as the whole philosophy of quantification and the use of numbers to express educational and psychological qualities. Such critical attack had the healthy effect of forcing testing enthusiasts to critically examine their assumptions and procedures and to broaden their approach to appraisal. During this period, attention shifted considerably from measuring a rather limited set of academic skills to evaluating a whole range of educational objectives. The evaluation report of the Eight-Year Study of the Progressive Education Association,[2] for example, describes efforts at gathering evidence on aspects of thinking, social sensitivity, appreciation, interests, and personal and social adjustment of students in the schools which participated in the study.

In many respects, this period of critical caution in testing has continued. The development of formal standards for judging tests and test manuals, as well as the series of *Mental Measurement Yearbooks* that contain critical reviews of a large number of published tests, have served to keep test users aware of the limitations as well as the strengths of the tests they use. While pressures for assessment increase, it is interesting to note that many local school districts do have testing programs which make use of standardized tests. In many cases, such programs have evolved over a period of years and reflect the combined judgment of teachers, guidance counselors, and administrators. Such programs are likely to continue. However, with the increasing realization that the contribution that standardized tests are likely to make to a local assessment program are limited, there is a growing tendency to seek out other kinds of assessment procedures that better reflect local objectives and instructional emphases.

Two trends worth noting are the use of locally developed tests and the selection of nationally available test materials that are judged to be germane to local objectives. In the former case, school districts are administering tests that have been constructed to local specifications by teachers and other school personnel. While such tests may be somewhat deficient in technical elegance, they yield information of high local relevance. As long as such tests are used primarily to describe the performance of groups of students rather than to appraise individual students, they can play an important role in local assessment efforts since they provide information that would probably not otherwise be obtained. In the case of judicious selection of nationally available test materials, local school districts are showing an increasing sophistication in their choice. Local school districts also tend to be increasingly selective in their use of such materials. This increasing selectivity appears to stem from a new level of concern about educational objectives and the relationship between objectives and testing procedures.

Another trend in the assessment of education at the local level is increased attention to affective outcomes. While educators at all levels have expressed concern about affective outcomes, there has not been a corresponding effort in gathering related evidence. It appears that educators are now beginning to systematically gather such evidence. Currently used measures of affective outcomes are often crude and indirect. For example, at the elementary school level, a single questionnaire item might be used to obtain an estimate of a student's attitude toward reading while at the high school level, attendance information might be used in making an inference about a student's disposition toward a school. Despite the highly questionable nature of such roughshod procedures for gathering information about affective outcomes, attempts are being made to gather information in this area. It is expected that such efforts will continue and that progress will be made in developing better measures of affective outcomes of educational programs.

As state educational assessment programs are carried out, local school districts will be receiving information as to how their students perform on various statewide measures. School districts will thus be in a position to make year-to-year comparisons on the progress of their students as well as building-by-building comparisons. One can also expect that comparisons between school districts will be made, whether they are warranted or not.

It can be expected that information from statewide assessments of education will be somewhat unsatisfying to school district personnel for three reasons. First, there will no doubt be the feeling that measures used in a statewide assessment program are not fully compatible with local objectives and curricular emphases. Second, school district personnel are likely to feel that information from a statewide assessment provides a rather incomplete picture of accomplishments (or the lack of them) at the local level. Third, local school personnel are apt to be dissatisfied with broad general measures that furnish little guidance as to specific areas of the instructional program that require strengthening. For example, if a sizable proportion of students in a particular school receive low scores on a general reading comprehension test given to the third grade, one knows almost nothing about what aspects of the reading program, if any, require modification. Such a lack of detailed information is apt to be a source of frustration at the school district and school building level.

It also seems unlikely that the results of statewide educational assessments will be fully satisfying to community residents. The pressures for some sort of educational accounting at the local level have increased so greatly in recent years that anything less than a determined effort at the local level to develop and carry out an assessment program will be considered inadequate. Although the demand for educational accountability has grown, it is not at all clear what kinds of information, or how it is gathered, organized, and presented, will satisfy this demand. This is one of the dilemmas which school personnel face at the local level. Even when they wish to be maximally responsive to their constituents, school personnel are apt to be somewhat uncertain as to what is wanted.

To be sure, there are some kinds of information that are routinely collected that can be used in an assessment program at the local level. Besides standardized test results, information on the proportion of students completing high school along with follow-up data on what they do afterward can be gathered and presented fairly easily. What additional information needs to be gathered for a local assessment program and how it can be used to satisfy accountability demands is largely an open matter. The dilemma of the local school district is thus also an opportunity to consider its educational values and to identify the kinds of evidence that will indicate the extent to which these values are being realized. Furthermore, the kinds of evidence that can be used in an assessment program at the local level need not consist exclusively of test data. For example, if teachers in a particular school district are consciously seeking to develop the reading interests of students, circulation figures from school and public libraries might be highly useful in documenting how well they are succeeding.

It is, of course, the responsibility of people at the local level to determine the particular educational values the schools should be emphasizing. Once this is decided, however, there are general procedures and techniques that can be used in an assessment program that are quite different from a testing program. The technique of item sampling, for example, can be usefully employed by a school district to gather information in a fraction of the time that would be required if every student were to be administered every question in an assessment instrument. Locally developed criterion-referenced measures (see Chapter 8), with or without item sampling, can also be used to furnish information with regard to both cognitive and affective outcomes of an educational program. Furthermore, since the object of an assessment program is to furnish information about fairly large units such as a class, a grade, a building, or an entire school district, rather than an individual student, some of the technical considerations involved in evidence gathering are substantially reduced.

Test publishers are responding to the new demands for tests that serve local school purposes more effectively. Some are developing criterion-referenced tests, and some are using their pools of test exercises to produce tests designed to specifications furnished by a local school system. Furthermore, some publishers are seeking to construct tests that are more closely related to classroom instruction, such as diagnostic tests. Teachers can employ such tests after having given a survey test in a particular subject to identify the specific achievements and learning difficulties of pupils. Test manuals are being developed that indicate sections of current textbooks in which the pupil will find material to study for those areas in which the diagnosis indicates he is having difficulty.

Many schools face a problem when they change their local testing program. Parents dissatisfied with the achievements of their children, and community members who are pressing the schools for evidence of effectiveness, are likely to view a change in the testing program as an effort of the school to find tests that will show the school to better advantage rather than believing that the school is honestly seeking tests and testing procedures that will help it improve its effectiveness. This dilemma should be faced, because the older programs are not furnishing the information needed by the schools and the public. One approach is to continue critical features of the old program while mounting a more effective one. This can be done without markedly decreasing the time students require for their studies.

Notes

1. Leonard P. Ayres, "History of the Present Status of Educational Measurements," *The Measurement of Educational Products,* Seventeenth Yearbook of the National Society for the Study of Education, Part II (Bloomington, Ill.: Public School Publishing Co., 1918), 11.

2. E. R. Smith and R. W. Tyler, *Appraising and Recording Student Progress* (New York: Harper and Row, 1942).

Part Six
Tests as a Means of Measuring Educational Programs, Methods, and Instructional Materials

12. The Use of Tests in Measuring the Effectiveness of Educational Programs, Methods, and Instructional Materials

Ralph W. Tyler

Since 1925 the accepted design for studying educational effectiveness has been, at some initial point, to give an achievement test called a pretest, and, at a final or later point, a comparable posttest. The gain in the mean score was taken as a measure of the educational effectiveness of the program, method, or instructional material. In case a pretest could not be given, the final scores could be compared with test norms or with the scores obtained from comparable groups not following the program method or material under study. Recently, however, the use of typical standard tests for this measurement has been seriously questioned on several counts.

Criticisms of Standard Achievement Tests

One criticism is that these tests do not properly reflect the educational objectives of the new program, method, or instructional material. Usually, new educational programs are constructed to gain certain new educational objectives, to alter the emphasis on earlier aims, or, perhaps, to achieve both goals. For example, the "new mathematics" programs devised in the 1960's included as a major objective the development on the part of the students of an understanding of and an ability to use ways of thinking characteristic of mathematical study. Although the new programs also aimed at some of the objectives of older programs, such as computational skill and the ability to solve everyday quantitative problems, they were not given the same emphasis. Hence, when standard tests in arithmetic were employed to measure the effectiveness of the new mathematics programs, they were sharply criticized because the tests did not include exercises that sampled the students' understanding of and ability to use ways of thinking characteristic of mathematical study.

New methods of teaching and new instructional materials, like new programs, are also commonly developed as a means of attaining new objectives or of giving new emphasis to older ones. Some programs are constructed and some methods and materials are devised to help solve a learning problem that has been identified as critical. For example, after World War II, oral-aural methods of teaching a foreign language were designed to support the new emphasis on oral-aural skills. Just before World War II, the recommended curricula primarily emphasized the development of reading skills. The design of behavioral modification methods (operant) conditioning and the accompanying materials in primary school reading were a response to the recognition of the critical problems encountered in teaching reading to so-called "disadvantaged" children.

The use of the common published achievement tests to measure the effectiveness of new teaching methods or of new materials that are focused on new objectives is criticized on the same ground as their use for new educational programs, that is, the tests do not properly reflect the educational aims being sought. Another criticism is made when these tests are used to appraise the effectiveness of programs, methods, or instructional materials designed to solve a critical learning problem. The charge is often made that the tests do not furnish a reliable sample of exercises appropriate for the students who encounter such a problem. For example, new programs, new teaching methods, and new materials are often designed to improve the learning of disadvantaged children. Typically, these children score in the lowest quarter of the distribution of scores on a standard achievement test. But the exercises found in most of these tests are clustered around the 50 percent level of difficulty, with fewer than 10 percent of the exercises below the 25 percent level. Usually less than 5 percent of the exercises in a typical standard test are at the difficulty level where most disadvantaged children would make correct responses. This is such a small sample of items that it cannot furnish a reliable estimate of changes in the performance of disadvantaged children unless the new program, method, or instructional materials help to effect an enormous improvement in these children's responses. Standard tests were not designed to provide reliable measures of change at the extremes of the distribution.

A third criticism is leveled when typical achievement tests are used to appraise new instructional materials. The claim is sometimes made that such tests have been largely built by writing items that use only the words or the modalities found in existing materials, and they only provide information about how well students have learned what is presented in older materials. If proper appraisals are to be made, the tests should enable students to show that they have learned important concepts, principles, skills, and so forth, independent of their embodiment in the instructional materials.

Achievement Test Construction Not Consistent with School Efforts

In order to examine these criticisms impartially, it is necessary to review the bases on which achievement tests are constructed. School achievement is a term commonly used to mean that students are learning what the school seeks to teach. Learning is usually defined today as acquiring new patterns of behavior through experience. The efforts of the school are focused on developing certain patterns of behavior that are considered important to help students participate constructively in society and realize more fully their own personal potential. The school curriculum is designed as a set of experiences that are expected to stimulate students to attempt these patterns of behavior, to afford them an opportunity to practice these patterns, to guide their efforts, and to continue the learning activities until the desired patterns of behavior have become established. The purpose of achievement testing is to ascertain whether, in fact, the students have acquired the desired behavior. A test presents situations intended to evoke the desired behavior and then affords an opportunity to record the performance. Since there are many situations in which a desired pattern of behavior can be expressed, a test can present only a sampling. The selection of situations (test exercises) is critical in constructing an achievement test since a biased or inappropriate sample will not furnish dependable evidence as to the adequacy of the student's behavior. The procedure commonly followed is an important source of criticism when available achievement tests have been used to measure the effectiveness of an educational program, a method of teaching, or a set of instructional materials.

The most frequent criticism, which was mentioned earlier, is that a given achievement test does not reflect the particular objectives of the educational program, method, or instructional materials. That is, the patterns of behavior that the test attempts to sample are not precisely the same as the patterns which the program, method, or materials are designed to help students acquire. For example, a program in language arts may be designed to help students write more fluently, with less restriction in content, while the achievement test used might be a sample of exercises involving primarily spelling, grammar, and punctuation. Or, as another example, the teaching method to be appraised might be planned to help students conduct inquiry in science, while the achievement test used might contain a sample of exercises primarily requiring recall of information about science. Tests designed for the national market are constructed to sample topics common to the curriculum of most school systems. For this reason they may not include exercises that reflect those behavior patterns that are the aims of new programs, methods, and materials. A less commonly noted variant of this problem occurs in the case of behavior patterns that require several years for adequate development. School programs differ in the learning sequences followed to help students acquire such patterns. For example, there are several different sequences used to develop reading comprehension in the primary grades. Some schools begin with a "look-say" method using a carefully controlled vocabulary to develop competence in word recognition before students are trained in phonics and other techniques for attacking new words. Other schools begin with a phonic or linguistic approach. A test designed for use in the first grade that properly reflects the curriculum sequence of a "look-say" approach would be inappropriate as a measure of what pupils had learned who were receiving initial training in phonics or vice versa. A test designed for use at the end of the primary grades is more widely appropriate, however, because most reading programs are planned, by the end of the third grade, to help students comprehend a variety of materials without highly restricted vocabularies. As another example, some arithmetic programs begin with counting and then addition, followed later by subtraction; others treat addition and subtraction together. In the early stages of developing number concepts and computational skills, the particular patterns of behavior practiced differ in different programs so that an achievement test used to measure the effectiveness of a program in helping students acquire this behavior needs to be carefully examined to see whether it really furnishes an adequate sample of exercises evoking the appropriate behavior.

The second criticism is derived from certain assumptions made in selecting test exercises. Probably because achievement tests were a by-product of testing for selection in World War I and because they were strongly influenced by assumptions made in intelligence testing, achievement test theory assumed that the outcome of school learning was the gradual development of abilities, and, at any one grade, these abilities were normally distributed among children. Actually, school programs are based on contrary assumptions. The school curriculum provides for a particular pattern of behavior to be developed at a particular time, and a strong effort is made to help all or most children develop this behavior at that time. For example, addition of whole numbers is presented and practiced at a specified period and not taken up every month or year. The concept of photosynthesis is also dealt with at a particular time in the science curriculum. Furthermore, each teacher tries to help all his pupils master the addition of whole numbers, and each teacher of biology tries to help all his students understand the concept of photosynthesis. In general, knowledge that a child acquires piecemeal over a long period of time is often learned incidentally. Schools typically do not focus major attention on such learnings. Yet this kind of knowledge is generally found to be normally distributed among children at a given age. For example, an item of general information that can be obtained from such varied sources as T.V., newspapers, magazines, and conversations is often found to be normally distributed among children of the same age, and the proportion of the age group that acquires this information increases with age. But this is not characteristic of the particular skills or facts systematically taught to a given age group. In such cases the distribution is highly skewed for that age, and there is not a gradual increase in the proportion of the age group that has acquired this behavior.

In the construction of norm-referenced achievement tests, such assumptions influence the selection of exercises that approximate the conditions, based on an initial tryout. Exercises are retained when the initial results show that children are normally distributed and when there is an increase in the proportion of correct responses from grade to grade. Furthermore, exercises used in the tryout are eliminated when the distribution of correct responses is highly skewed or when there is not a significant increase in proportion from grade to grade. This procedure makes it likely that the selected exercises are not those on which instruction has been focused but, more probably, items that children learn incidentally. The exercises eliminated after the tryout are more likely to be those toward which major instructional effort has been directed.

The use of these assumptions in constructing norm-referenced tests leads to a common misinterpretation of the norm "grade level." What laymen think it means when a report states that a student is at the fourth-grade level on an achievement test is that the student has acquired some major fraction of the behavior patterns that the school is seeking to teach in the fourth grade. But it does not mean this at all. It means that his test score was the same as the median or mean score of all fourth-grade children in the norm group. In many cases the items answered correctly were not typical of the behavior emphasized in the fourth-grade curriculum of the school in which the pupil was enrolled. Norm-referenced tests are not composed of reliable samples of the things that children are being helped to learn in a given grade but, rather, samples of exercises on which children of a given grade differ markedly in performance. The things that most children are learning in that grade are likely not to be included in the test sample because of the item selection procedures.

The third criticism was that typical achievement tests include too small a sample of exercises appropriate for appraising the learning of children who markedly deviate from the average. Many new educational programs have been developed to improve the learning of pupils whose learning has been inadequate. For example, hundreds of new programs have been designed help disadvantaged children whose test scores are far below the mean of the distribution. If the tests are to measure improvements in the learning of disadvantaged children, the items on which they would be expected to improve would be the "easier" ones—that is, the ones which 75 percent or more of the norm group answer correctly. But the method of item selection maximized the number of items which about 50 percent of the norm group answered correctly because those items provide the greatest discrimination in placing pupils on a continuum from highest to lowest score. On most standard tests there are less than 5 percent "easy items," or those answered by 75 percent or more of the norm group. There are so few items at the level where disadvantaged children can be expected to be learning that changes in their test scores due to improved learning cannot be distinguished from those due to chance variations in performance on so few items. If the effectiveness of an educational program, teaching method, or a set of instructional materials designed to aid the learning of a special group like disadvantaged children is to be measured, tests are required that include a reliable sample of the behavior that the pupils are being helped to learn. At present, this usually necessitates the construction of new tests that are properly focused on the specific pattern of behavior.

A fourth criticism is related to the third. A teaching method or a set of instructional materials is commonly designed to improve learning significantly, but not spectacularly. A real improvement of 5 percent to 10 percent in the learning of students is often desired. To measure such differences in the learning of children would require a precision of measurement that is not usually attained or even attempted survey tests. Since survey tests (most standard tests) are usually administered no oftener than once a year and since most schools believe that the time they devote to survey testing should be kept at a minimum, the tests are designed to furnish scores sufficiently reliable to identify learning increments taking place in a year but not those that might occur in a fraction of a year. Hence, most survey tests cannot provide information about the differential effectiveness of teaching methods or instructional materials unless the differences are great.

Measuring Differential Effectiveness

In order to produce a test that can be used to measure the effectiveness of a teaching method or a set of instructional materials, it is necessary to obtain exercises that sample adequately the several patterns of behavior that students are being helped to learn, and, if necessary, oversample the behavior that is thought to be uniquely aided by the method or the materials. If the method or materials are to be compared with others, the test should sample in similar fashion any additional patterns of behavior that the others are aimed to develop so that information can be obtained on the relative effectiveness of the different methods or materials in developing each of the several patterns of behavior that are the aims of one or more of the methods or materials. For example, one method of teaching American history in the 11th grade is to assign small teams of students to investigate features of life characteristic of their grandparents' generation, each team covering one area of life such as the home, economic activity, political life, play, and leisure, securing data from interviews with senior citizens as well as from printed materials. Each team is expected to prepare a written report and to present an oral one for discussion and criticism of the class as a whole. The effectiveness of this method is to be compared with that of textbook reading and discussion.

The test developed for this comparison sampled behavior 1) involving the use of historical concepts in explaining the differences between their grandparents' time and the present; 2) recalling information gained in study about life in the two periods; 3) writing clear and well-organized expositions of a feature of life at the turn of the century; 4) making a bibliography to guide those who might want to investigate this period. Note that the first two sections of the test involved patterns of behavior emphasized by the teacher using textbook reading and the discussion method while the third and fourth sections represented additional objectives considered important by the teacher using the team-investigation method. In each section the test included an adequate sampling of the particular behaviors that students were expected to develop in this part of the course activities and, thus, it furnished a basis for the precision of measurement required to appraise relatively small increments of learning.

Measuring Changes in Behavior

There is another problem involved in assessing the effectiveness of an educational program, method, or set of instructional materials— that of measuring changes in behavior. At the beginning of a program many students have already acquired some of the desired patterns of behavior or some parts of the patterns. For them, the question is, did they learn additional desired patterns, or did they complete behavior patterns already begun? Did the educational means being tested aid the student in going beyond the point where he began? The simplest way to answer such a question would seem to require a measure of the student's relevant behavior patterns at or near the beginning of his participation in the program or the method or in his use of materials, and again at the end. To measure change requires two or more measures at different points in time.

Some of the problems involved in using tests to measure changes in patterns of human behavior have been discussed by social scientists in earlier publications. The report of a symposium on this subject was published in 1963.[1] More recently, Ronald Carver summarized the difficulties as follows:

1. Existing psychometric devices have been designed and developed to reflect accurately and efficiently individual differences, and this makes them of questionable validity when measuring changes within individuals or differences between groups.
2. Item selection techniques are largely responsible for rendering the traditional psychometric yardstick inadequate when measuring change.
3. It is a common procedure to interpret differences or changes on norm-referenced measures as accurately reflecting differences or changes in the variable supposedly measured by the device; yet recent theoretical models would suggest that this interpretation is grossly erroneous in most instances.
4. Statistical significance is not a sufficient condition for asserting the importance of a difference or a change.
5. Currently, there is a method which purports to be able to recalibrate existing test scores on a scale that allows absolute amounts of change to be measured, and this method deserves the attention of evaluation researchers.[2]

Continuing with his discussion of the problem of measuring change, Carver illustrated interesting aspects of the problem in a section entitled "Developing Measures of Change," which is reprinted here from the volume *Evaluative Research, Strategies and Methods* (Pittsburgh: American Institutes for Research, 1970), 55-59, with the permission of the publishers.

I first became aware of the knowledge gap in measurement practice when I attended a group meeting on a large social-educational evaluation project. A questionnaire was to be developed to measure the effects of a film project on a small town in California. Someone suggested a question that might be used on the questionnaire. Another person responded that he thought the question would be pertinent but that it probably would not produce much variability, i.e., before the treatment almost all respondents would answer the question in the same manner. This kind of criticism reflects high competency in traditional theory which, unfortunately, is irrelevant for measuring change. The perfect item for demonstrating change would be one with zero variability on the pretest and zero variability on the posttest, but a difference between the two sets of responses.

Whereas variability is a prerequisite for reliability and validity in norm-referenced measurement, it is irrelevant and often detrimental to the measurement of change in criterion-referenced measurement.[3] Evaluators should disregard the distracting principle of variability when developing test and questionnaire items to measure change. This does not mean, however, that license can be given for the disregard of reliability and validity.

Reliability of a criterion-referenced measure or an absolute measure scale depends upon replicability, but replicability is not dependent upon variability. If the alternate form reliability of a measuring instrument is estimated by administering it twice to the same group, and all individuals make exactly the same score or respond the same way on both forms, then it is perfectly reliable. However, the reliability coefficient calculated using traditional methods would result in a zero reliability estimate for the instrument, since the variability between individuals is zero. Popham and Husek[4] have noted the inadequacies of the traditional approach to reliability and have expressed a need for the development of appropriate indices.

It would seem that the reliability of a criterion-referenced device would be relatively easy to estimate in most practical situations. Two forms of the device might be administered to a sample of the target population, and the percentage that met the criterion on one form could be directly compared to the percentage that met the criterion on the other form. The degree to which these two percentages were equal would be the degree to which the instrument was reliable. The reliability of a single form of a criterion-referenced device could be estimated by administering it to two comparable groups. The percentage that met the criterion in one group could be compared to the percentage that met the criterion in the other group, and the degree to which these two percentages were equal would be an estimate of the degree to which the device was reliable.

For an absolute measurement scale, simple techniques could also be devised for estimating reliability. Below is a rough and ready statistic that might be used to estimate the reliability of an absolute measurement scale.

$$\text{Average Absolute Error} = .707 \ \frac{\sum\limits_{I}^{N} d_i}{N} \tag{1}$$

where d_i = absolute difference (without regard to sign) between the score on Forms A & B of the instrument for individual i

N = total number of respondents

The above formula expresses the average perpendicular distance between the data points and the line of perfect correspondence between the two sets of scores. The constant .707 results from the use of the x and y data coordinates to calculate the perpendicular distance from the data point to the line of perfect correspondence.

The above statistic is independent of between individual variability and gives a meaningful estimate of the absolute size of the error involved when substituting one measuring instrument for the other. This statistic could be used for individually scaled items as well as an entire test or questionnaire scale. The units designated on the instrument itself would seem to provide an inherently meaningful reference unit, and the error in Equation 1 is expressed in the same units. A measuring instrument that has an Average Absolute Error less than one unit would be an unusually reliable test. Yet, the relative reliability would seem to depend upon the error in relation to the maximum possible error in absolute terms. A statistic that would express this type of reliability would be:

$$\text{Relative Absolute Error } (\%) = \frac{e_a}{R} \times 100 \qquad (2)$$

where e_a = Average Absolute Error from Equation 1

R = Range of possible score units; maximum possible score minus minimum possible score.

As a concrete example of the use of the above statistics, the raw data on the aforementioned reading test[5] was substituted into Equation 1 and the resulting Average Absolute Error was 5.6 score units. Since the scores on this test could vary from 0 to 100, the Relative Absolute Error (e_a) was 5.6 percent. For various reasons the above reliability statistics may not have popular support. Yet it is hoped that their presentation has further demonstrated the marked departure of this approach from its norm-referenced counterpart.

The validity of criterion-referenced or absolute measurement devices depends upon the ingenuity of the individual developing the measurement device and does not depend upon a correlation with some other variable.[6] For a criterion-referenced device, the developer must be able to devise a meaningful criterion. The organization that is presently striving to measure educational progress in the United States is going to great lengths to develop sound criteria.[7] For example, they want to be able to report the percent of 9-, 13-, and 17-year-olds, as well as adults, who know the name of the President of the United States. They will measure change in terms of the percentage differences among the various age groups as well as change in five-year increments into the future.

Another example of a meaningful criterion used by this organization is the ability to read, with comprehension, a paragraph from the front page of a newspaper. This specific measurement procedure would probably not discriminate well among the reading abilities of college sophomores, for example, but it will probably be quite good as an indicator of future progress in education.

Of major concern when evaluating change is knowing how to gauge the size of changes or the units of change. Wright[8] has suggested that this problem be solved by establishing anchor points or groups that establish the meaning of units. For example, he suggests that a special group of persons or a special group of items be used to establish a reference unit; this unit might be the scores from a failing group. The better defined and more meaningfully communicated, the better the reference unit. In the area of curriculum evaluation, Scriven[9] has suggested that control curriculums be established to help evaluate change. That is, he suggested that a "dummy" curriculum might be developed during a summer by college students with little formal knowledge or guidelines, and this curriculum would help evaluate the changes produced by an experimental curriculum.

Another example of how this type of procedure helps interpret changes or differences comes from a reading experiment by Carver.[10] An experimental reading typography was compared to a regular typography to see if the experimental one facilitated reading rate and/or comprehension. To help interpret the results, another control typography was administered which had no punctuation or capitalization. A decrement or change produced by a format which has no punctuation or capitalization is a meaningful kind of change which is readily interpretable. If this format produced little or no effect in relation to the regular type of reading format, then it would be reasonable to infer that something was wrong with the experiment or the measurement devices. If this format did produce a change, then the amount of this change could be compared to the size of the change produced by the experimental format. This latter comparison facilitated a meaningful interpretation of the importance of the experimental results.

In summary, when developing measures of change for evaluation, do not rely completely upon traditional measurement knowledge and theory. Variability may be detrimental to the reliability and validity of criterion-referenced measures, and traditional statistics for estimating reliability and validity must be reanalyzed for relevance. Meaningful measures of change must be tied to meaningful reference points, and this often requires great ingenuity on the part of the evaluator conducting the research.

Notes

1. Chester W. Harris (ed.), *Problems in Measuring Change* (Madison: University of Wisconsin Press, 1963).

2. Ronald P. Carver, "Special Problems in Measuring Change with Psychometric Devices," in *Evaluative Research, Strategies and Methods* (Pittsburgh: American Institutes for Research, 1970), 55.

3. W. J. Popham and T. R. Husek, "Implications of Criterion-Referenced Measurement," *Journal of Educational Measurement* 6 (Spring 1969), 1-9.

4. *Ibid.*

5. Ronald P. Carver and C. A. Darby, Jr., "Analysis of the Chunked Reading Test," unpublished report (Pittsburgh: American Institutes for Research, 1970).

6. Popham and Husek, *op. cit.*

7. Ralph W. Tyler, "The Objectives and Plans for a National Assessment of Educational Progress," *Journal of Educational Measurement* 3 (Spring 1966), 1-4.

8. Benjamin Wright, "Sample-free Test Calibration and Person Measurement," in *Proceedings* of the 1967 Invitational Conference on Testing Problems (Princeton, N.J.: Educational Testing Service, 1967), 85-101.

9. M. Scriven, "The Methodology of Evaluation," in R. W. Tyler, R. M. Gagne, and M. Scriven (eds.), *Perspectives of Curriculum Evaluation,* American Educational Research Association Monograph Series on Curriculum Evaluation (Chicago: Rand McNally, 1967), 39-84.

10. Ronald P. Carver, "Effect of a 'Chunked' Typography upon Reading Rate and Comprehension," *Journal of Applied Psychology* 54 (June 1970), 288-96.

Part Seven
Tests and Privacy

13. Invasion of Privacy

Richard M. Wolf

Invasion of privacy in connection with the use of tests has received considerable attention during the past several years. Willingham, in an introduction to a special supplement to the *Journal of Educational Measurement* on "Invasion of Privacy in Research and Testing" listed the following observations as likely contributing or underlying influences for the emergence of the issue at this time in history:

First, social concern for individual dignity and privacy has been greatly sensitized by the civil rights movement. In this context, identification of personal characteristics which set individuals apart constitutes invasion of privacy because such identification may invite invidious comparison or discrimination.

Second, current social movements and accompanying "great society" programs have heightened the demand on behavioral scientists to work on social problems which require investigation of precisely those characteristics usually felt to be private. To the extent that these movements can be regarded as one dramatic phase in a continuous process of social levelling, then there is reason to expect a continuing tension between the desire to minimize personal distinctions (which protects privacy) and to equalize opportunity (which requires investigation of inequality).

Third, greatly increased financial resources for research have not only increased the level of activity but have also made large projects possible. Being highly visible, the large research project is more subject to public criticism— sometimes for various reasons rationalized partly in the name of privacy. And there are recent indications that the involvement of public funds evokes a special public concern for privacy.

Fourth, the concerns are greatly heightened by the advent of computer technology. With modern methods of data processing, identification, and retrieval, information once released by an individual may find its way into many hands. The danger lies in gradual erosion of the individual's right to decide to whom he wishes to disclose personal information.

Fifth, there have been fundamental changes in behavioral science during the past two decades with reference to its theory and methods. Psychology, in particular, has tended to move from relatively abstract and innocuous studies to research that seems to matter—to society and to the subject. Ironically, some present research which causes concern in the context of individual privacy may be attributed indirectly to public criticism of the irrelevancy of much behavioral research in past generations.

Sixth, it seems unlikely that the public makes clear distinctions between invasion of privacy in different fields for different purposes. Thus, concerns with respect to research and testing undoubtedly are enhanced by a backlash from electronic eavesdropping, supersecret intelligence activities, and other worrisome mechanisms of social control.[1]

The issue of invasion of privacy has perhaps been most cogently set forth by Goslin[2] who noted, "A test is a potential invasion of privacy because personal information is made available to others. Very important values in American society suggest that individuals have the right to decide to whom and under what conditions they will make available to others information about themselves." However, as Goslin also points out, "Correlative to this point . . . is the fact that participation in society carries with it certain obligations and responsibilities. Further, certain groups clearly have the right to demand information from those who want the privilege of group membership." For example, the "right" of a state government to determine whether an individual can pass a driving test before being issued a driver's license is unquestioned. However, as one moves from the above example to others that are less mundane, the waters become murkier. Consider the following actual samples cited by Berelson:

Item 1: College students in a psychological experiment are placed in a manipulated, deceptive situation in which a single person's judgment is placed against the unanimous judgment of his fellows, who are all collaborators of the investigator. As a consequence, some students give in to the group's views, deliberately erroneous though they are, with resulting loss of self-esteem and some humiliation in front of their peers.

Item 2: Students in junior high school are given the Minnesota Multiphasic Personality Inventory, including questions that some of them, and more of their parents, consider disturbing and inappropriate.

Item 3: Without parental knowledge or consent, public school students are asked detailed questions about how their parents get along, and how their parents treat them.

Item 4: College students surreptitiously observe the behavior of members of their own families when TV commercials come on the home screen in order to see how people really respond to commercials of different kinds, duration, and spacing.

Item 5: Subjects respond to the face value of the questions in an instrument that purportedly has projective value, so that the subject is presumably revealing aspects of his own personality without his knowledge or consent. Or subjects take a test on male-female inclinations, where no single item is offensive, but the total pattern may be.

Item 6: The proposal is made that substantially all collection of information by public agencies include the individual's social security number, so that with modern electronic equipment, a large body of information can quickly be brought together on the same individual from the various sources in which it was initially collected.[3]

The above are only a few examples that suggest the dimensions of the issue involved in the invasion of privacy. That a fundamental issue is involved cannot be denied, although, like many public issues, a number of side issues have cropped up both in public and in professional discussions.[4] These, however, will not be dealt with here.

There appear to be five major aspects to the issue of invasion of privacy. These are: (1) respecting the dignity of the person tested, (2) permissibility of deception, (3) the rights of an institution to obtain information necessary for achieving its goals, (4) the special status of school children, and (5) limits on the freedom of scientific inquiry.

Respecting the Dignity of the Person Tested

This aspect of the issue involves the nature of questions asked of examinees. Consider the following questions that not infrequently turn up on questionnaires:

What is your father's occupation?

How many years of schooling has your father had?

About how many books are there in your home?

Questions such as these have frequently been asked in order to gain some indication of a student's socioeconomic status. Similarly, questions involving the student's feelings and home life have sometimes been asked. In some cases the information obtained has been used in an accountability program that wishes to take into account the home conditions of students while, in other cases, information about possible maladjustment has been used to single out individuals for help. The rationale behind asking such questions is that the community interest is served by such information if constructive use is made of it. On the other hand, there is the principle that no one should be forced to testify against himself. There is also, as Cronbach[5] points out, "The parents' right not to have *their* privacy invaded by such questions as 'Do your parents quarrel frequently?' "

Whether educators and psychologists could fulfill their professional functions without asking questions that might be viewed as objectionable by many people cannot be easily answered. One opinion on the matter is given by S. R. Hathaway, one of the authors of the Minnesota Multiphasic Personality Inventory (MMPI). The MMPI has been severely criticized in connection with its use in selecting government employees, notably Peace Corps applicants. Hathaway's position is, in part, "It is obvious that, if we were making a new MMPI, we would again be faced either with being offensive to subgroupings of people by personal items they object to or, if we did not include personal items and were inoffensive, we would have lost the aim of the instrument."[6]

The picture, however, may not be as bleak as Hathaway seems to feel. A study by A. Fink and J. N. Butcher,[7] which informed subjects about the MMPI in advance—how the instrument was constructed and how the scales were used—revealed that the informed subjects, according to a posttest questionnaire, considered the test situation to be *less* of an invasion of privacy than individuals who took the MMPI under standard test conditions. Interestingly, there were no appreciable differences in the profiles of results between the standard and informed groups of subjects who had been assigned at random to one of the two groups. It would seem that greater use of informed consent will be made in the future, especially if it can be shown that the quality of the information obtained from testing does not suffer.

Permissibility of Deception

There are many occasions in which the test constructor tries to outwit the subject so that he cannot guess what information he is revealing. From the test constructor's point of view this is necessary since he wishes to ascertain information that the individual might not be able to furnish if it were sought directly. A number of personality inventories fall into this category as, incidentally, do many medical diagnostic procedures.

As a general principle, many educators and psychologists suggest introducing a testing procedure with as full and as frank a discussion as possible. This works quite well with many kinds of instruments, such as interest inventories, where the object of the procedure is to provide the individual with information that he would willingly allow others to know if he were able to furnish it directly. However, it would be extremely difficult to give a full and frank introduction of a test that attempts to determine a person's style of work (for example, dependency) without alerting him and probably causing him to alter his typical behavior so as to be seen in the best possible light. Certainly, the first example cited from Berelson could probably not have been carried out if deception had not been used.

There is no easy answer to the issue of deception. Educators and psychologists who are involved in the development and use of tests often justify the use of deception on the grounds that it is necessary in order to obtain information for worthwhile purposes such as helping a maladjusted individual, protecting society by preventing unstable people from occupying critical positions, and so forth. However, if the results of a testing situation in which deception was employed are used in making a decision which the individual considers adverse, such as denial of admission to a particular program or institution, there are potentially serious legal and ethical questions. Entrapment is an explicitly illegal procedure in the United States. To what extent the use of deception in testing can be considered a form of entrapment has yet to be determined.

Rights of the Institution

Institutions have particular functions to perform and goals to be attained. Schools, in particular, are concerned with helping individuals learn. In order to fulfill this function, they need to have information. It is widely accepted, for example, that schools have a right to require students to demonstrate proficiency in school subjects before according them advanced status through promotion or graduation. As one moves away from the achievement domain, it becomes less clear what information schools require in order to carry out their main function. For example, do schools have the right to require students to demonstrate their general intellectual ability apart from their proficiency in specific subjects? One might argue, on the one hand, that schools do indeed have the right since without it they are prevented from fully realizing their central mission. On the other hand, it is argued that such information is not germane to the main goal of the schools. (The issue of whether intellectual ability test data are used for the benefit or to the detriment of the individual is another issue entirely and will not be dealt with here.) Indirect support for this position can be found in the 1971 Supreme Court Decision in the case Griggs *et al. v.* Duke Power Company where the Court ruled against the use of "broad and general testing devices" in employment situations and held that, ". . . any tests used must measure the person for the job and not the person in the abstract."[8] This is not to suggest that the testing of intellectual ability in a school setting is in any way illegal or unethical. What is being suggested is that schools need to carefully determine what kinds of test information they need to enable them to realize their goals.

Special Status of School Children

School children constitute a captive audience. Attendance laws require them to go to school usually until at least the age of sixteen. For the most part, the school child does not have any choice as to whether he will or will not take tests that are given by the school. This lack of freedom makes it especially important for schools to determine that their testing needs are in the best interest of the child and do not exploit his special status as a student.

Closely related to the issue of the right of the school to collect test data is the issue of the release of test information. Does the school have the right to withhold test information from the student and his parents? Conversely, what rights do students and parents have to know what information the school possesses about them? In at least one case (New York State), the courts have held that parents do have the right to know the information contained in the pupil's permanent record file.

Limits on Freedom of Scientific Inquiry

Behavioral scientists are faced with a dilemma. On the one hand, they wish to find out as much as possible about man and his behavior. Such knowledge is not only valuable in itself, but it can also be of service in solving social problems. It is surely in the public interest to know what kinds of people become delinquents, what kinds of influences produce a James Earl Ray or a Martin Luther King, Jr. To find out, behavioral scientists must be free to inquire into these phenomena. On the other hand, the kind of information that is collected can represent a real invasion of individual privacy, especially if deception is practiced in collecting the data. Also, if data collected for a research purpose were to be used for another, unrelated purpose, there would be very serious ethical and legal problems. For example, if data gathered on the behavior of student leaders as part of a study of campus rebellion were to be used by college administrators to decide whether student leaders should be expelled, fundamental constitutional issues could be involved. While the above example may seem extreme, it is not farfetched. The development of advanced computer technology for the storage and retrieval of information makes such a prospect not only conceivable but fairly easily accomplished. Furthermore, as Cronbach[9] points out, "Coding of records is not a full safeguard. Identity can be detected by matching facts from the coded questionnaire with other facts that are openly recorded."

Some Emerging Trends

While it is not possible to predict what will happen in the future with regard to the issue of invasion of privacy, it is possible to comment on what is happening at present. First, discussion of the issue of invasion of privacy in both professional and public circles has increased enormously in the past few years. Newspaper and magazine articles dealing with the subject have increased substantially. The *American Psychologist* devoted an entire issue to the topic in 1966, and the *Journal of Educational Measurement* put out a special supplement in 1967. General textbooks on testing such as Mehrens and Lehmann's *Measurement and Evaluation in Education and Psychology*[10] now routinely devote several pages to the issue. Textbooks in personality testing *per se* typically cover the topic in some detail. The net effect is increased sensitivity among professionals. A second development is that professional organizations are beginning to issue position statements with regard to psychological assessment and public policy. In 1970 the American Psychological Association's position statement maintained, for example, that,

The right of an individual to decline to be assessed or to refuse to answer questions he considers improper or impertinent has never been and should not be questioned. This right should be pointed out to the examinee in the context of information about the confidentiality of results.[11]

A third development is evident in the behavior of researchers. Debriefing of subjects at the conclusion of an experiment is generally commonplace. Also, there appears to be greater care being taken in the selection and administration of testing procedures. Greater precautions are being taken in the handling of test information. In some cases, answer sheets containing detailed response data are being destroyed as soon as summary statistics are produced while in other cases elaborate coding procedures have been developed to try and conceal the identity of the individual respondent.

In summary, there is markedly increased sensitivity concerning the issue of invasion of privacy. Greater efforts are being made to explain the purposes of testing to examinees either before or after testing them. Also, various kinds of self-restraint are being practiced as one of the costs of doing business in the behavioral sciences. Whether such self-imposed restraints, guided by the pronouncements of professional associations, will suffice in helping to resolve the issue of invasion of privacy remains to be seen.

Notes

1. W. W. Willingham, Foreword to "Invasion of Privacy in Research and Testing," Supplement to *Journal of Educational Measurement* 4 (Spring 1967), 1-2.

2. D. A. Goslin, "Standardized Ability Tests and Testing," *Science* 159 (February 23, 1968), 854.

3. Bernard Berelson, Introduction to "Invasion of Privacy in Research and Testing," Supplement to *Journal of Educational Measurement* 4 (Spring 1967), 5-6.

4. L. J. Cronbach, *Essentials of Psychological Testing* (third edition) (New York: Harper and Row, 1970), 510-11.

5. *Ibid.*

6. S. R. Hathaway, "MMPI: Professional Use by Professional People," *American Psychologist* 19 (March 1964), 204-10.

7. A. Fink and J. N. Butcher, "Reducing Objections to Personality Inventories with Special Instructions," *Educational and Psychological Measurement* 32 (Winter 1972), 631-39.

8. Supreme Court of the United States, Willie S. Griggs *et al.*, Petitioners *v.* Duke Power Company, No. 124, October Term, 1970 (March 8, 1971), 1-12.

9. Cronbach, *op. cit.*

10. W. A. Mehrens and I. J. Lehmann, *Measurement and Evaluation in Education and Psychology* (New York: Holt, Rinehart and Winston, 1973), 665-67.

11. American Psychological Association, "Psychological Assessment and Public Policy," *American Psychologist* 25 (March 1970), 264-66.

Conclusion

In Retrospect

Ralph W. Tyler

The development of standard tests for appraising human behavior is sometimes selected as the most important contribution that has thus far been made by behavioral scientists. Certainly, it has contributed markedly to the systematic, objective study of human behavior and has furnished important concepts and principles used in describing and explaining behavior in scientific terms. However, particular tests were developed for particular purposes, using particular assumptions and techniques of the times. As times have changed, tests are being used for new purposes in schools that are operating under different assumptions. As the discrepancies between the old and the new have become apparent, issues have arisen questioning and challenging the uses of tests and their value for the new purposes to which they have been put. These issues have arisen most sharply in five contexts: the drive to extend civil rights to all sections of American society; the growing efforts to make education effective for all children and youth; the call for assessment of educational institutions; the need to appraise new educational programs, methods, and instructional materials; and the concern for protecting the private life of the individual in this interdependent, increasingly crowded society.

Tests were originally constructed to serve in the sorting and selection of individuals. Now, they are to be used to help the individual in his efforts to learn. Educational opportunities are no longer to be restricted to those who progress most easily through the educational process as it has been conducted. Tests are to be used to help the school and the teachers to work effectively with children whose behavior patterns are diverse.

Tests were originally constructed using the school or college as a standard of correctness so that test items were rated for validity in terms of their correlation with success in school or college, or with teachers' marks. Now tests are to be used to assess the school or college, and to appraise the effectiveness of educational programs, methods, and instructional materials.

Attitude tests and other measures in the affective domain were developed when the school or college was commonly viewed as a surrogate parent for its students. Now, the right of an educational institution to ask questions that might invade the privacy of the individual child is seriously questioned. Clearly, a critical examination of the use of tests for particular purposes is needed so that the devices used to measure human behavior are appropriate to, and consistent with, the purposes and the contemporary situation.

The response to criticism of testing is not to give up efforts to assess human behavior. Individuals today need more not less information about their behavior than in the past in order to make constructive use of their varied opportunities not only in education but in all aspects of life. If teachers are to facilitate the learning of their students, a better understanding of the student's progress and difficulties in learning is needed. If schools and colleges are to deal effectively with the tasks they are asked to assume, they must know much more about their students, teachers, programs, procedures, and materials. Obtaining more and better information requires the development of new instruments as well as stopping the inappropriate use of older ones. Testing will go on because it is needed, but it must and can be improved.